Parenting
shelf

Parenting
shelf

LEARNING
CHAMPS

The book that will teach you how to learn faster and remember facts better.

We would like to thank Jenny Greenwood who has acted as educational consultant on CHAMPS.

Jenny was a teacher for many years and is responsible for teacher training in 'Accelerated Learning and Study Skills' at Dulwich College in London. She is an associate trainer with 'The Industrial Society' where she regularly runs the 'Brain Fitness for Business' course. She is also involved with The Graduate Business School in Cape Town where she runs a successful combination course, 'Brain Fitness and Accelerated Learning for Business'.

Publishing Director: Chester Fisher
Educational Consultant: Jenny Greenwood

Art Direction and Design: Tessa Barwick
Illustration: Debi Ani
Photogaphy: Steve Lumb

Published in 2002 by Sterling Publishing Co., Inc.
387 Park Avenue South, New York, NY 10016

ISBN: 0-8069-9032-5

First Published in the UK in 2001 by Learning World, an imprint of Chrysalis Books plc, 64 Brewery Road, London N7 9NT

Printed in China

Picture credit: Robin Kerrod 58b

The Authors

Colin Rose

Colin Rose is one of the world's foremost experts on learning. He is the inspiration behind Learning CHAMPS, and its co-author. He is best known as the man who took the priciples of Accelerated Learning out of the theoretical realm of university research and introduced them to the public. Founder and Chairman of Accelerated Learning Systems Ltd, he is a consultant to many corporations and universities and in demand as a speaker on learning and education at international conferences and symposiums.

He is also a member of the initial steering committee of the UK's Campaign for Learning. This is an initiative of the Royal Society for the Encouragement of Arts, Manufacturers & Commerce, supported by the British Government and Industry. A father of four, Colin lives in Buckinghamshire, England with his wife Joanna and his two children, Alexander and Catherine.

Anne Civardi

Anne Civardi is the author of over 40 innovative fiction and nonfiction children's books. A founder member of Usborne Publishing, she has also written books for many major publishers, including MacMillan, Penguin, Chronicle, Time Life, and Scholastic. She has recently completed a series of Family Activity Guides for the National Gallery in London.

Anne has teamed up with Colin Rose, in conjunction with The Campaign for Learning, to produce CHAMPS, as a book, as well as an interactive internet version. She is a passionate advocate of encouraging children to improve their confidence, self-esteem, and learning skills. Currently, Anne is developing a new series of self-help books that she believes will be a huge benefit to anyone from the ages of 8 to 80!

Anne was brought up in Africa but now lives in London with her husband Todd and their three children, Jake, Sophie, and Amber. When she is not writing, she is a sculptress!

Contents

WELCOME TO CHAMPS

Step 1 C = CONFIDENT TO LEARN

Step 2 H=HOME IN ON THE FACTS

Step 3 A = ACTION!

Contents

Learning CHAMPS and you

Learning CHAMPS will help students acquire the most important skill of all: the ability to learn any subject effectively and quickly, and to remember what they have learned.

In today's fast-paced world, *what* students learn can become outdated. But *how* to learn is a skill that will last them a lifetime. It is surely *the* underpinning skill for raising achievement. Yet until now we have rarely taught this skill. We teach *what*—but rarely *how*.

Learning CHAMPS fills that gap. It is based on fascinating recent discoveries about the brain and how people learn. These have led to the recognition that each student has a way of learning that suits them best—a preferred learning style.

If students can be helped to recognize those preferences—and acquire the techniques that best match their own learning style—they become better and more confident learners.

FOR STUDENTS

Learning CHAMPS provides you with a multitude of proven techniques for motivation, goal-setting, concentration, understanding, note-taking, memorizing, stylish writing, and revising—plus successful exam strategies.

FOR PARENTS

Learning CHAMPS gives you a practical way to help your child succeed at school and far beyond. To become a self-motivated learner—capable of coping with a competitive modern world where information is plentiful and easily available—so long as he or she knows how to use it effectively and creatively.

FOR TEACHERS

Learning CHAMPS helps you develop students who are self-motivated, self-managed learners who, because they understand how they learn, are better able to collaborate positively with you in class.

In short, to become CHAMPION LEARNERS!

WELCOME TO CHAMPS

If you know HOW to learn,
WHAT you learn becomes easier.

- What if you could learn anything you wanted *fast* and *easily*? How would that make you feel?

- What if you could *remember* difficult things like history dates, math formulas, or science facts more easily?

- What if you could start getting *better results* at school within the next few days?

- What if you could learn how to *concentrate* and *listen* better?

- What if you could *get yourself going*, or *motivate*, yourself to get down to work at any time?

- What if you felt really *confident* to tackle any school subject, even the ones you don't think you're very good at?

Did you know? CHAMPS will train your brain to get to the top and to become a better, faster learner.

Well now you can! This brilliant book will teach you all the things you need to become a learning CHAMP—something that will help you for the rest of your life—at home, at school, and at work.

At school you get taught lots of different subjects, like math, English, science, and history. But you're not often taught *how* to learn them. Yet learning is like playing a sport, or playing a musical instrument. It's a skill. And CHAMPS is going to teach you this most important skill of all.

The best techniques for you

Does your face look the same as your friends' faces? Are your fingerprints the same? No! And neither is your brain.

Your brain is as individual as your fingerprints or face. Since you learn with your brain, you won't be surprised to know that you have a unique way of learning that suits your unique brain best.

When you use the techniques that match the way your brain learns best, you'll be learning in the way that's most natural to you.
- *Because it is natural, it's **easier**.*
- *Because it's easier, it's **quicker**.*
- *And because it's quicker it's more **fun**.*

That's just what **CHAMPS** will do for you! It'll teach you the learning techniques that match the way your brain likes to learn best. So if you're already a good learner—you'll get better. And if you find learning a bit of a struggle, your work will get easier and your marks will get better.

You're already a good learner!

Guess what? You may not know it, but you *are* already a very good learner.

YOU'VE LEARNED TO DO ALL KINDS OF THINGS, LIKE:

- learn a language—English!
- ride a bike
- read
- swim
- make friends
- tell the time
- play a sport
- write a story
- use a computer
- play a musical instrument

How did you learn them? Did it take practice? Did you have to learn the right technique?

When you first learned to ride a bike, you had to learn the technique. You had to ride just fast enough not to fall off, and learn how to balance. You stuck at it, because you wanted to learn it. It seemed difficult at first, but once you learned the technique it was easy, wasn't it?

Learning to do anything well is a matter of having the right techniques and that always needs a bit of training—just like sports CHAMPS have to train hard if they want to get to the top.

your brilliant brain

You really have got what it takes to learn anything you want—*your amazing brain.* It's a brilliant piece of equipment that can think far better and is much more creative and imaginative than the most powerful computer—anywhere. Let's see just how brilliant it really is!

Your brain cells

It's hard to believe but you have about 100 billion brain cells. That's right—

100,000,000,000

—which is almost 20 times the population of the whole world!

It means that you have *more* than enough potential brainpower to learn anything you want! But you need lots of help to get the most out of your brain.

A brain cell looks a bit like a tiny octopus. Lots of little threads, called *dendrites*, branch out from the body of each cell. When you *see* or *hear* or *do* something, it creates a thought or impression. These thoughts travel out (by a form of electricity!) from a brain cell, and along one of those little dendrites.

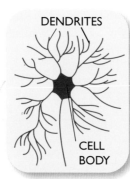

DENDRITES

CELL BODY

BRAIN CELL

When it gets to the end of that dendrite, the thought jumps over a tiny gap to the next dendrite and so on. Sometimes thousands of brain cells will be connected by just one experience or thought.

Making connections

Every time this chain reaction takes place, new connections are formed between brain cells. If you repeat the same thing over and over again, some of these connections become permanent. When that happens, you are able to do something automatically—without having to think about it.

That's why you can remember how to do so many things, like writing or reading. You made *permanent* connections through repetition.

Coach's Hot Tip

The more you use your brain, the more connections you make between your brain cells. The more connections between your brain cells, the cleverer you become!

Your brain cells only give you the possibility to be intelligent. Your actual intelligence depends on the number of connections you make between your brain cells.

School work really can make you more intelligent!

You make these connections by having lots of interests and living life to the fullest—through things like reading, learning, sports, music, art, and travel—by using your brain and thinking in different ways.

Unstimulated brain   Stimulated brain

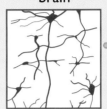

Did you know?
You'll never get too old to make new connections. You just have to keep learning and looking for new experiences.

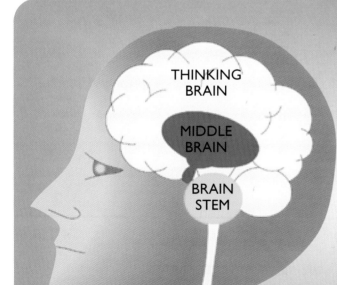

THINKING BRAIN

MIDDLE BRAIN

BRAIN STEM

Three special parts

Did you know that you can think of your brain as having three special parts?

Your thinking brain

Is your intelligent brain. It stores memories, learns, thinks, and creates.

Your emotional or middle brain

Controls your emotions, moods, and feelings. It helps decide what you will remember.

Your brain stem or primitive brain

Controls your breathing, your heartbeat, and sleep. It reacts to danger and stress.

Your brain stem or primitive brain

At the base of your skull, you have a rather simple, primitive brain. It's this part of your brain that makes sure you keep breathing and your heart keeps beating.

When you're worried or frightened about something, your brain stem sends alarm signals to the part of your body that makes you ready to run away from danger or fight. This is called the *"flight or fight"* response.

You need to know how to relax and calm yourself to become a learning CHAMP! You'll find out how later.

Your primitive brain also makes you angry or uncomfortable if someone crowds too close to you or wants to take something that is yours. *Has that ever happened to you?*

Your primitive brain is sometimes called your *reptilian brain* because that's how a reptile's brain works. When you see a person bullying someone or being aggressive, you could say they are behaving in a reptilian way.

Going blank

When you're frightened, worried, or stressed out, your body produces a chemical called *adrenaline*. It makes your heart beat faster and your muscles tighten up.

When this happens, the thinking part of your brain can shut down and your mind can go *"blank."*

- *Has this ever happened to you?*
- *What else happened?*
- *How did your stomach feel?*
- *Could you think properly?*

Your emotional or middle brain

The middle part of your brain controls your health (by controlling your immune system). It also controls your feelings and emotions, such as joy, sadness, anger, happiness, or jealousy. And it's responsible for deciding just what you are going to remember.

WHAT SORTS OF THINGS DO YOU REMEMBER?

dull things	exciting things
happy things	bad news
funny things	boring things
frightening things	surprises
interesting things	rude things
things you don't like	beginnings
colorful things	middles
difficult things	endings

You probably remember exciting things that mean a lot to you or involve strong emotions better than those that are boring and don't mean so much to you. Things like the time when you first learned to swim or ride a bike, went on an exciting vacation with your family, or were given something you really wanted.

So when you do something to make your school work more colorful, dramatic, or visually exciting—you make it more memorable.

Your thinking brain

Make a fist with your hand. Now wrap your other hand over the top of it. Pretend your wrist is your *brain stem* and your fist is your *middle brain.* The hand wrapped over it is your *thinking brain.*

This third brain is incredible. It contains everything you will ever need to learn and remember anything you want. So long as you know how!

It's the brain's "*thinking*" center, where problems are solved, questions are answered, messages are sorted out, and decisions are made about what you should do!

Remember!
Your thinking brain can shut down or not work so well when you are frightened or worried.

Side-by-side

Your *thinking brain* is divided into two halves which specialize in different things. Some people tend to use the left side of their brains more when they tackle a problem. They are happy to build up their knowledge of a subject bit-by-bit, in a slow and logical manner.

Did you know? The two halves of your brain are joined together and they work as a team.

The big picture

Let's say you're singing a song. Your left brain will deal with the words and your right brain will deal with the melody and the music. You probably know how to sing lots of songs without even trying!

THE RIGHT HALF SPECIALIZES IN:

patterns

art and music

creativity

intuition ("gut" feelings)

the melody of a song

seeing the whole picture

2324 ÷ 896 =
bonjour

THE LEFT HALF SPECIALIZES IN:

facts and details

numbers

symbols

step-by-step logic

the words of a song

speech, language, and words

Other people tend to use their right brains more. They're the sort of people who get bored with getting the detail too early. They want to find out what something is all about straight away—they want to see the "*big picture*".

If you are doing a jigsaw puzzle, it's easier to look at the "*big picture*" on the box lid—with your right brain—while you're tackling the detail of the pieces—with your left brain.

Coach's Hot Tip

You learn better and more easily when you use the left and right sides of your brain together.

That's why it makes sense to use music and rhyme, words and pictures, as well as searching out the detail as you learn. It makes sure your whole brain is taking part in the learning!

Why positive feelings help you learn

Your emotional, middle brain is actually called your *limbic system*. It's such a big influence on how well you learn because information comes into your brain through one of your senses. So you either *see* it, *hear* it, *feel* it, *taste* it, or *smell* it.

That information goes first to your *emotional brain,* which acts like a "central switchboard". If it decides the information is worthwhile, it switches it up to your *thinking brain.*

Does it make you feel good?

Remember, your middle brain also controls your emotions, or feelings. So, when the new information is sent to you in ways that make you feel good about it, you can learn well and remember well. Now think of the teachers who teach you in an exciting and positive way?

- *Are they enthusiastic about what they are teaching?*
- *Does it make a difference to the way you learn and remember things?*

Why negative feelings stop you learning

When you are feeling negative, frightened, or under stress, your middle brain may stop the information it is receiving from ever reaching your thinking brain. Your middle brain blots it out. This can make your mind *"go blank"*.

003.5< 005…

Some people feel worried or threatened by learning new things. Because they feel they are bad at learning, they feel threatened. Because they feel threatened their thinking brain receives less information, so they really do learn less. It's like a vicious circle.

That's why, when you are worried, you may suddenly realize that you have been staring at a page without taking anything in! So it makes sense to know how to be calm and confident before you even start to learn.

Did you know?
When you learn something that includes colors, pictures, games, and sometimes music, you feel more positive and excited about it and so you learn it better.

CHAMPS action plan

Right, so now you've learned a lot about how you learn—things like:

- How you feel is a big influence on how well you learn.
- Everyone has favorite ways to take in information.
- You have more than enough brain-power to learn anything you want. The secret is knowing how to use all of it properly. And that's what this book is all about—techniques to make the most of your brain.

Now it's time to start finding out about those techniques, but remember you don't have to learn them all at once. Start with the ones that suit your way of learning best.

The more you read CHAMPS, the more useful techniques you will discover. There are six important steps to follow. Start at Step 1 and read right through to Step 6. With all that incredible information you'll soon become a CHAMPION LEARNER too!

YOUR SIX STEPS TO SUCCESS

C **onfident to learn—**   **STEP 1**
Teaches you to be relaxed, confident, fit, and enthusiastic before you start learning. If you are stressed, or don't believe you can do it, you won't learn well.

H **ome in on the facts—**   **STEP 2**
Shows you how to take in the facts to suit the way you like to learn best, and make those facts easy to remember.

A **ction!—**   **STEP 3**
Here you'll find out how to explore and think about what you are learning—with one or more of your 8 intelligences.

M **emorize it—**   **STEP 4**
Trains you to memorize just a few key ideas of what you have learned. Once you have done this, you will find it easy to remember it all.

P **rove you know—**   **STEP 5**
Makes sure that you have really understood what you've learned by testing yourself.

S **it back and think—**   **STEP 6**
Tells you how important it is to think about how you learned. The aim is to improve, not just what you know, but how you learn. That way you'll become a learning CHAMP.

Step 1

CONFIDENT TO LEARN

If you believe you can succeed, you will!
But if you convince yourself you're going to fail,
you probably will too!

Introduction

Right, so now you've found out all about the power of your brain and what CHAMPS will do for you. It's time to take your first step to becoming a learning CHAMP.

Step 1 of CHAMPS will show you how to get your brain ready to learn. And it will help you build up your confidence and belief in yourself.

You will also find out that to learn better, faster, and more happily you have to look after yourself.

To do this, you need a balanced diet, regular exercise, somewhere comfortable and warm to work, and at least eight hours sleep every night.

You also need to be relaxed, motivated, and enthusiastic.

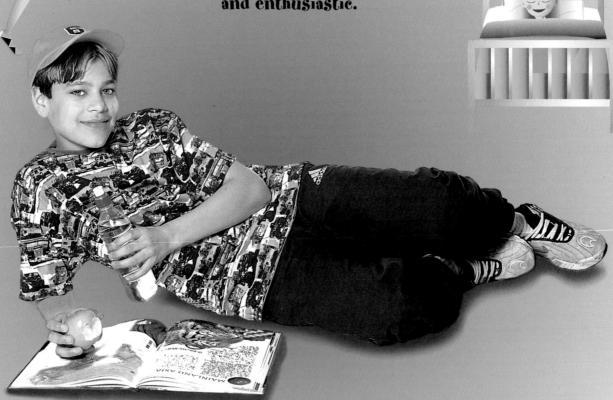

Believe in yourself

How you feel about learning is very, very important. Top athletes don't just dash out on to the track. First they mentally prepare themselves for action. They motivate themselves and picture the race in their mind. This is called *visualization*. It's the same with learning.

To learn well, you first need to be in the right state of mind. You need to feel good about yourself and really believe you can learn anything you want.

Whether you think you can, or whether you think you can't, you're probably right!

Did you know? It's easy to change a negative (−) to a positive (+) with a simple stroke of the pen.

If you truly believe you will succeed, you usually will—in the end. But people who don't believe in themselves usually fail—in the beginning!

A positive state of mind makes you much more able to learn or tackle anything new.

THINK ABOUT THIS!

You learn more slowly when:

✗ you are worried or stressed

✗ you have convinced yourself you can't do something

✗ you are bored

✗ you are tired, hungry, or thirsty

✗ you are learning in a way that doesn't suit your style of learning

You learn fastest when:

⭐ you are relaxed and feel positive and motivated

⭐ you work in a comfortable place

⭐ you believe you can succeed

⭐ you learn in a way that suits you best

⭐ you use all your learning senses (you'll find out how later)

Say it, feel it, do it!

Now you're going to learn a secret that will help you for the rest of life. But first, try this!

THE LEMON TEST

Imagine you're in the kitchen. You raise a lemon to your nose. It has a sharp lemony, citrus smell, doesn't it?

Now you cut the lemon in half. The two halves fall apart and you see drops of lemon juice dripping out.

You raise the lemon to your nose and smell that sharp lemony smell. Now you bite into it and taste the sharp, sour flavor.

Did your mouth water? Almost everyone's does. But of course there was no "*real*" lemon—only the one in your mind.

Yet your mind directly affected your body. Your imagination—*by itself*—was able to make your mouth water.

Coach's Hot Tip

So here's the secret! What you imagine strongly and clearly enough in your mind often comes true.

Don't worry!

Unfortunately it's the same with negative thoughts as well as positive thoughts.

You've first got to SAY it, and FEEL it—then you'll DO it!

That's why a nightmare can make you wake up feeling really frightened. It wasn't real but it had a real affect on your body. You imagined you were frightened and so you became frightened.

Being worried is just the same. You sometimes worry about imaginary things, but the feeling it creates in your body is real enough.

That's why if you believe you will succeed, you set yourself up to succeed. But if believe you'll fail, then you set yourself up to fail too.

Be positive

Do you ever talk to yourself?
Do you chat away inside your head?

Everybody has a little voice inside their
head that seems to talk to them whatever
they're doing.

This inner voice might say things like,
"Oh, no, I'm going to mess this up", or
"I feel good and I'm going to get it right".

It's good so long at it is saying positive things.
But it's not so good when it's saying bad
or negative things.

THINK ABOUT THIS!

Positive statements are called **affirmations**.
Here are the sorts of affirmations learning
CHAMPS might say:

⭐ I am a learning CHAMP!

⭐ I am a math marvel

⭐ I am a super speller

⭐ I am a marvellous musician

⭐ I am a great geographer

⭐ I am fantastic at French

⭐ I am excellent at English

Pick one or two and repeat them to yourself
over and over again during the next few weeks.
Or better still make up your own.

**Make a habit of talking to yourself in
a very positive way. Talk to yourself as if
you were already successful at whatever
you're tackling.**

You can also repeat your *affirmation* to
yourself whenever you're faced with a tricky
situation. Write it down and put it in a place
where you will see it every day.

I am a great musician

I am a great musician

**Did
you know?**
The best time to repeat
your affirmations is
when you are in bed
and drifting off to sleep.

Picture it in your mind

Did you know that you can "*program*" your brain to learn well and to be successful? You do it through something called *visualization*.

Visualization means creating pictures in your mind. It's when a word or story comes alive in your head. You did it when you imagined the lemon—remember!

Did you know?
Sports coaches and trainers believe that 5 minutes of visualization could be worth 2 hours of training!

Program your brain for success in 6 easy steps

Step 1

Picture in your mind a time when you were really successful, perhaps you got a good grade in an exam or won a race.

Step 2

Remember everything about it. *What did you see at that moment? What did you hear? What did you feel?*

Step 3

When you have really and truly remembered that particular success and how good you felt about it, think of one word that sums it up—maybe something like "YEEEESSSS". This is your "*cue*" word.

Step 4

Sit up straight. Pull your shoulders back. Look upward and take a deep breath. Don't you feel different already?

Step 5

Close your eyes and clench your fist. Now remember your big success again and say your "*cue*" word to yourself over and over again. That felt good, didn't it?

Step 6

Try visualizing this moment of success over the next few days. Repeat the five steps and you'll find that you'll be able to return to this good and positive feeling anytime you want. You need to choose a quiet time to practice and to do it often. But it's really worth it!

'YEEEESSSS!'

Coach's Hot Tip

Creating a "positive" picture in your mind over and over again programs your mind to look for ways to make those mental pictures become real.

Relax!

Remember you learned that if you feel stressed, threatened, or frightened, your thinking brain can shut down and your mind can go *"blank"*? So it's easy to understand that to become a learning CHAMP, you need to know how to relax and keep calm.

Stress isn't best!

Do you sometimes feel tense or stressed? Does it make your neck and shoulders sore? Does it stop you from thinking properly?

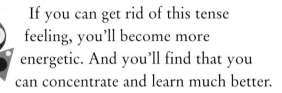

If you can get rid of this tense feeling, you'll become more energetic. And you'll find that you can concentrate and learn much better.

What makes you feel stressed?

Look at the list below. Do you recognize any of the statements?

There are all sorts of things that might cause you stress, but what makes one person tense may not make another person tense.

THINGS THAT CAN CAUSE STRESS:

- ✖ people being mean or bullying you
- ✖ sitting in front of a computer for too long
- ✖ having too much work to do
- ✖ not having time to do your homework
- ✖ being unfit
- ✖ putting things off until the last minute

HOW TO STOP THAT TENSE FEELING:

- ★ plan and organize your time
- ★ talk positively to yourself
- ★ do some relaxing exercises
- ★ plan your goals
- ★ eat sensibly
- ★ get enough sleep
- ★ listen to relaxing music

Relax!

Deep breathing

It's hard to imagine but your brain weighs about 4 pounds, which is only about 4 percent of your body weight. Yet it takes up 20 percent of the oxygen you breathe in. So, before each school lesson (and throughout the day if you need to), close your eyes and breathe deeply, like this, for just a minute or two.

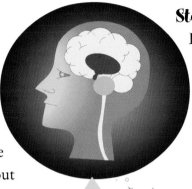

Guess what?
When you breathe well, you supply your brain with plenty of oxygen, which makes it work better!

Step 2
Breathe in through your nose and let this balloon slowly fill up. Hold your breath for a few seconds.

Step 3
As you slowly breathe out, say the word "*c a l m*" and let the balloon become smaller and smaller until there is no air left in your tummy at all. Do 6 deep breaths like this.

NECK ROLLS

Step 1
Hunch your shoulders as high as you can up to your ears. Breathe in really deeply. As you breathe out, drop your shoulders and dangle your arms by your sides.

Step 2
Pull your shoulders down as far as you can. Look up and stretch your neck, making it as long as possible. Now, let go and relax. Repeat this 4 more times.

Step 1
Sit on the floor or in a chair with your back and spine straight. Look upward and let your jaw fall loose. Put your hands on your stomach and imagine there's a big balloon inside it.

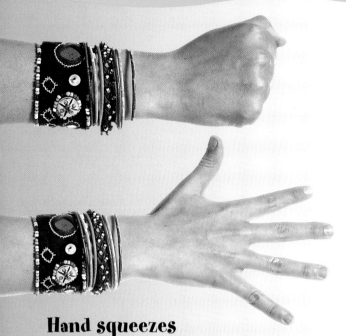

Hand squeezes

Squeeze your hands into a really tight ball.
Stretch open your hands. Spread your fingers
and make them grow as long as you can.
Now, drop your hands. Let them go.
Do they feel really heavy?
Repeat 6 times.

Coach's Hot Tip

Deep breathing, neck exercises, and
an upright straight spine all allow blood,
oxygen, and energy to pass freely between
your body and your brain!

The total chill out!

Lie down on the floor. Relax your feet
until they are so heavy you can't lift them.
Imagine they're in a bowl of warm water.
Then imagine this warm feeling going up your
legs and slowly filling your whole body—your
bottom, your stomach, your hands, your arms,
your neck, and your head.

THE STRESS PRESS

Whenever you feel a bit stressed or panicky,
press your fingers gently on the two points
just above your eyebrows. It will relieve the
stress and help you concentrate again.
Try massaging behind your ears too!

Take a brain break

Did you know that the longest you are able
to concentrate properly is about 30 minutes?
So every 30 minutes or so take a *"brain break"*.
It need only be a minute or two, but you will
learn better after you've had a short rest.

Try drinking
a glass of water or doing one of
the exercises you've just read about.
You'll come back refreshed
and ready to learn!

Set your goals

Imagine two archers. One takes careful aim at the target, the other just looks casually and shoots. Who do you think is more likely to succeed? *The fact is; you won't hit a target that you don't aim for or can't see.*

That's why successful people set themselves clear goals or targets. It's something to aim for and it helps concentrate their minds.

You may have one particular goal you want to achieve, or you may have lots of different goals. Some may be things you can do in a short time, others may take much longer, or may even be things you hope to do when you leave school.

"What's In It For Me?"

Once you have set yourself a goal, really think about what you'll gain from achieving that goal. What difference will it make to your life?

Say to yourself:
"What's In It For Me?"

Then think of the things you might achieve.

YOU MIGHT:

★ be much more likely to pass an important exam

★ be proud of yourself

★ get a great report card

★ get a place in a sports team

★ be able to speak another language when you travel

Guess what?

Reaching the goals you set yourself gives you a sense of achievement and makes you feel good about yourself.

If you picture in your mind what your goal is going to do for you, you'll find that your brain will be much more willing to help get you there. And you won't mind working hard to achieve that goal.

Write them down

The best way to achieve a goal is to think it out carefully and then write it down. You'll be much more likely to succeed if you do.

I will learn 1,500 new French words by the end of the year

6 GOOD REASONS TO WRITE DOWN YOUR GOALS:

1. You'll have to think about your goals in more detail.
2. By putting them on paper they become more real.
3. It sends a message to your brain that you mean business.
4. You can see when you've reached them.
5. You can refer to them from time to time.
6. You'll feel good when you check them off.

Remember!
If it's a really important goal, put it on paper and stick it up where you will see it every day.

Write down your goals now and when you hope to reach them. Then check each one off once you have achieved it.

My goals	I will achieve by	Done
1. I will get 20 out of 20 for my spelling test	Jan 12th	✓
2. I will get an A in my science exam	March 2nd	✓
3. I will become fit	June 9th	

Picture your goals

Have a look at your written goals and visualize how you'll feel when you've achieved them. *What will you look like? How will you feel? What will people say to you?*

Coach's Hot Tip

Don't get your goals and your wishes mixed up.

When you say "*I wish I was better at math*", what you really mean is, "*I'd **like** to be better, but I can't be **bothered** to make the effort*".

If you wish for something, it's just something you hope for—you're not **committed**. But when you say "*I will be better at math*", you are **telling** your brain to start acting!!

Make an action plan

An action plan is simple. It's just a list of the main things you'll need to do to achieve your goals.

ACTION PLAN FOR EGYPTIAN TEST

To do	Deadline
1. Who ruled Egypt (pharaohs)?	Monday
2. Why were pyramids built?	Tuesday
3. The importance of the Nile river	Wednesday
4. Egyptian feasts	Thursday
5. Egyptian houses—flat roofs, mud bricks	Friday
6. The gods of Egypt—temples	Saturday
7. Reward myself	Saturday

All action lists have a date on them. That's when you'll have done the job. It's called a *deadline*. Setting *deadlines* means **you** are in charge—and that makes you feel good.

Coach's Hot Tip

Remember! It's a good idea to check your action plan every day.

3 GOOD REASONS WHY YOU SHOULD REWARD YOURSELF:

1. Rewards make you feel good. You want to get that feeling again, so you keep going.

2. It sends a signal to your brain to get in the habit of doing it right.

3. It's better for you to motivate yourself than rely on others to motivate you.

Reward yourself!

It's important to take notice of each of your successes and congratulate yourself on them. You could even buy yourself a present, such as a new CD or a ticket to the movies, when you reach a goal or when you reach a step on the way to achieving one.

So, from now on, when you notice you're doing something well, or have reached a goal, reward yourself or give yourself a pat on the back.

Tell someone else about your goals. Then you'll become more motivated and feel even more determined not to let yourself down.

Write down your successes so you can look back on each one.

Get organized

It's much easier to get down to your homework if you are not only feeling relaxed and positive, but also if you are organized. Otherwise, you can waste a lot of time and energy.

Your life is measured by time. So wasting your time is wasting your life!

Managing your time

Managing your time is as important as memory or exam skills. And it's just as easy. It helps you to do the things that need to be done at the right time. It also helps you keep in control and keeps you feeling positive.

Planning your weekly homework

Look at each of your projects. Figure out how much time you need to:
* *research the facts you need to find out*
* *write up the answers*
* *check it, edit it, and/or improve the way it's laid out*

Then make a simple daily timetable, like the one below. Write down when you will do each piece of work. It's your *timetable.*

A TIMETABLE HELPS BECAUSE:

* you'll feel less stressed
* you'll have more free time
* you get your work in on time
* you are controlling your time —it's not controlling you
* you know when you'll be working and when you have free time
* you'll feel good about your work and yourself
* there will be no more last minute stress

Remember!

Stick to your plan and always check off each task as you finish it. It'll give you a sense of achievement and motivate you.

MON	TUES	WED	THURS	FRI	SAT
Math 70 mins ✓	Research Greeks 40 mins ✓	Review spelling 45 mins ✓	Check Math 20 mins ✓	Write up Greeks 45 mins ✓	Chill out
	Swimming ✓		Music ✓	Sports	

Get organized

Your learning kit

Here's a list of things you always need while you are learning. It's useful to have them at your fingertips. So get them ready in advance in one place.

Coach's Hot Tip

Plan your learning kit now. Then you won't waste time later looking for the things you need.

YOU'LL NEED THINGS LIKE:

- colored pens and pencils
- notepaper—plain and lined
- folders and files with dividers
- sharpeners and erasers
- highlighters

- scissors
- index cards
- calculator
- "post-it" notes
- white out
- glue

- paper clips
- stapler
- hole-puncher
- calendar
- tacks
- sticky tape

Your learning corner

It's not just the tools you need, you also need a special place in which to learn—even if it's just a corner of your dining room table.

Try to find an area where you can make yourself comfortable (that's not too noisy or busy)—a place where you can always do your best work.

For some people, the right background music helps to make them more alert and concentrate better. Especially if it's something without words that's not too loud!
Sorry CHAMPS!!

Guess what?
Having your own learning area is important and will affect the way you learn.

YOUR LEARNING CORNER MIGHT INCLUDE:

★ a desk or table and a comfortable chair

★ good light and the right temperature

★ pictures of what you would like to be or do

★ positive statements or your affirmations

★ photos of people who are important to you

★ pictures that give you a good feeling

★ reminders of past successes like:
  • certificates and awards you have won
  • photos, cups, or medals
  • good reort cards
  • your best piece of work

Fit to learn

Do you want to learn better, faster, and more happily?
Well, you know that you need to have goals, you need to be motivated, and you need to know how to relax.
Another very important part of learning is being *fit to learn*.

Guess What?
Food, combined with oxygen in the air you breathe, is the fuel that helps you to grow and gives you energy. Water is essential too!

Since your body affects your mind—just as your mind affects your body—you've got to feed your brain and body properly to be fit to learn!

WHAT MAKES YOU FIT TO LEARN?

★ Getting plenty of oxygen—that's why deep breathing is so important.

★ Eating brain food.

★ Drinking plenty of water.

★ Getting lots of exercise—to help your brain grow and repair itself.

★ Sleep—the best get rest!

Coach's Hot Tip

A fit brain helps you to remember what you have learned and makes it easier to review for tests and exams.

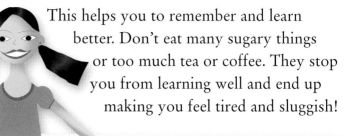

Brain food

To become a learning CHAMP, you need to eat a good balance of different types of food. Carbohydrates and fruit give you loads of energy. This helps you to remember and learn better. Don't eat many sugary things or too much tea or coffee. They stop you from learning well and end up making you feel tired and sluggish!

Eat loads of green vegetables. They're full of magnesium, which helps you cope with stress and supplies your body with fiber.

Fish is really good for you and it keeps your muscles in good working order.

Proteins, like eggs, lean meat, fish, milk, beans, and nuts help your body grow and repair itself.

Lean red meat or beans are full of iron, which keeps your blood healthy.

All kinds of fruit are full of vitamin C and nutrients that protect your health.

Carbohydrates, like bread, rice, pasta, potatoes, cereals, and bananas. Bananas are loaded with potassium, which helps your memory. Carbohydrates make you feel full of vim and vigor.

Drink plenty of water!

Guess what?
You need water for electrical connections in your brain cells to happen, and for digestion and breathing.

Exercise

Exercising every day keeps you fit, gives you loads of energy, makes you more alert, and helps your brain work better. Choose something you enjoy, like riding a bike, swimming, or playing soccer. You need to exercise quite hard for at least 20 minutes three times a week.

WHEN YOU EXERCISE:

Your heart gets stronger so it pumps blood around your body more efficiently.

Your muscles get bigger, which makes you stronger.

It gives your mind a break.

You breathe more deeply and take in more oxygen.

You relax and become less stressed.

You feel more enthusiastic and energetic.

It helps you think more positively.

Remember!
Always warm up before you start exercising by stretching your muscles. And "cool down" when you finish.

Guess what?
10-14 year-olds need at least 10 hours sleep a night. 14-18 year-olds need about 9.

Coach's Hot Tip

Relax before you go to sleep. Don't force yourself to work too late and become overtired.

The best get rest

It's hard to believe but you spend about a third of your life asleep! It sounds a terrible waste of time, but it's necessary for your brain to relax and recover from the work its done during the day.

While you sleep, your brain sorts out problems and the answers to difficult questions inside your mind. It's also a time when you dream, which is another important part of learning.

While you sleep, the hormone that helps you grow is distributed around your body. This builds muscles and tones and repairs your skin.

Now scientists have also discovered that you go over new things you have learned while you sleep—so a quick scan of your notes about an hour before you sleep is an easy and effortless way to review!

THINGS TO HELP YOU SLEEP:

zzZz stick to a regular bedtime

zzZz don't drink coffee or tea too late

zzZz exercise during the day

zzZz listen to some quiet music

zzZz have a bath before bed

zzZz read a good book in bed

Learning map

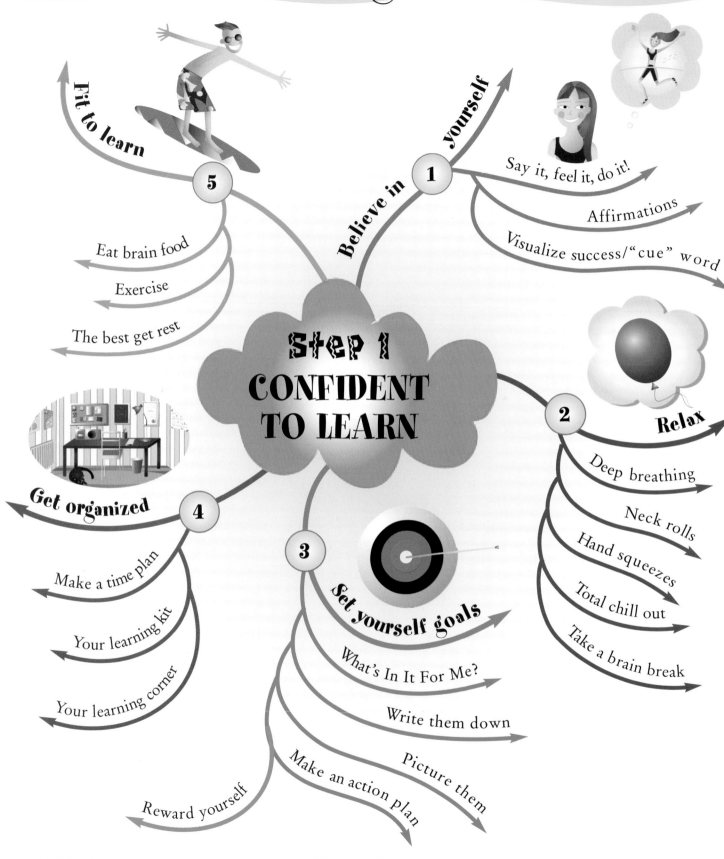

Step 1 CONFIDENT TO LEARN

1 Believe in yourself
- Say it, feel it, do it!
- Affirmations
- Visualize success/"cue" word

2 Relax
- Deep breathing
- Neck rolls
- Hand squeezes
- Total chill out
- Take a brain break

3 Set yourself goals
- What's In It For Me?
- Write them down
- Picture them
- Make an action plan
- Reward yourself

4 Get organized
- Make a time plan
- Your learning kit
- Your learning corner

5 Fit to learn
- Eat brain food
- Exercise
- The best get rest

Step 2

HOME IN ON THE FACTS

All knowledge is just the answer to a question!

Introduction

In Step 1 of CHAMPS you found out how important it is
to get ready to learn—to picture success in your mind,
have a fit brain and body, set goals, and know how to relax.

Well, that was all to get yourself prepared.

Now it's time to find out how to actually learn.

Step 2 of CHAMPS will show you how to take in the facts to suit
the way you like to learn best. And it will give you some handy tips
that will help you to absorb
information easily.

What's the big idea?

Trying to learn anything new without first getting an idea of what it's all about is a bit like doing a jigsaw puzzle without looking at the picture on the box. When you have the "*big picture*", it's much easier to fit the pieces together and make sense of the details! It's the same when you learn anything new. You need to find out what the main idea of a subject is before you explore it in detail.

Scan it!

The best way to find the "*big picture*" or main idea of a book you're reading is to **scan it first**.

Once you've scanned through your book, you'll end up with a pretty good picture of what you're studying and you'll have a sense of direction about it.

But remember, you haven't got the detail yet. So it's best not to jump to any conclusions or think you know it all until you have explored the subject fully.

HOW TO SCAN:

- First flick through your book slowly to get an idea of what it's all about.
- Look at the index.
- Look at the chapter headings.
- Look at the pictures.
- Look at any summaries at the beginning or end of chapters.
- Stop and glance at anything that really interests you.

Coach's Hot Tip

Once you have the "big picture" or main idea, everything else falls into place and starts to make sense.

Guess what?
When you flick through a newspaper, your eyes scan the headlines to decide what you want to read.

Take it step-by-step

How do you eat a sandwich or hamburger?
Do you put the whole thing in your mouth?
No, that would be horrible—you wouldn't taste it properly, you wouldn't enjoy it, and it may make you choke!
You take one bite at a time.

It's the same with school work. When you learn bite-sized pieces, you can build up a lot of information easily and quickly, and enjoy it.

Coach's Hot Tip

It's best to take learning a step at a time—learn a small chunk before you tackle the next one.

TRY THIS:

1. Start on something as simple as the chapter headings of a textbook you are reading.

2. Look for one topic that really interests you—this will lead you on to other areas.

3. Learn one page at a time. Check the end of each page to show you've really understood what you've read.

4. Use small "post-it" notes to divide up your textbook into little bite-sized chunks.

Guess what? You could easily find 15 spare minutes a day for a bit of extra learning just waiting at a bus stop.

Use your spare time

In 15 minutes a day you could easily learn 5 words of French. Write the English on one side of a small piece of card and the French on the other. Guess what? In under a year you could have learned over 1,500 words!

How do you eat an elephant?

One bite at a time!

sauter to jump

What do you already know?

MICROBES
(bacteria and viruses)
ENTER BODY THROUGH:
1. skin and eyes
2. digestive system
3. respiratory system
4. reproductive system
5. vectors
   (mosquitos,
   fleas, etc.)

Jot it down

Right, so now you've got the "*big picture*", it's helpful to jot down what you already know. Don't write too many words. It's best just to keep to the most important (*key*) words that help you remember.

Start by jotting down the *key* words of what you learned in your last lesson. You can do this for any subject you want to review easily.

Spending a minute or two jotting down the *key* words of what you know helps because:
- *It starts your brain thinking.*
- *It shows you what you don't know—so you know what you need to find out !*

Did you know?
Key words are usually nouns (names of people, places, or things). Because they are nouns they are easy to remember.

Connect to your last lesson

Your teachers don't just dream up your lessons on the spot! Each lesson is part of your syllabus (what you need to know by the end of the year). And, more than likely, they will have prepared in advance a plan of what they are going to teach you for every lesson. Each lesson connects in some way to the one before, and the one after.

A great way to remind yourself of these connections is to take a quick look back over your notes on the last lesson to see what you were doing. It gets your brain ready for the new stuff, and it's a useful minute of revision.

Coach's Hot Tip

Every lesson connects in some way to the one before— and the one after.

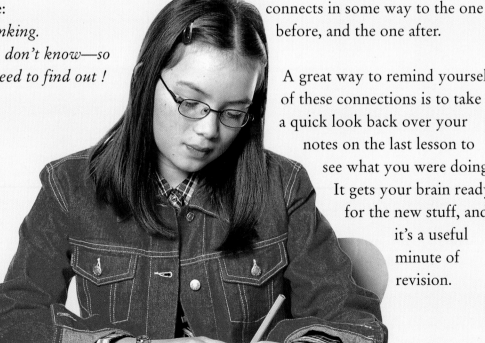

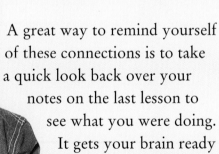

Ask yourself questions

Have you ever found your mind wandering or found yourself getting bored while you were trying to learn something?
Of course you have—everyone has!
Being unable to concentrate and getting bored are two big reasons that stop you from becoming a learning CHAMP. So here's what you do! It's one of the most important learning techniques of all.
YOU ASK YOURSELF QUESTIONS!

WHAT? WHY? WHEN? HOW? WHERE? WHO?

Say you were about to study an event like the first landing on the Moon, you might ask yourself these sorts of questions:

What . . . does the Moon's surface look like?

Why . . . do astronauts have to wear spacesuits?

When . . . did the landing take place?

How . . . did the astronauts train for their space mission?

Where . . . did the spaceship Apollo 11 blast-off from?

Who . . . were the first men to set foot on the Moon?

OR THESE KINDS OF QUESTIONS:

Is there any gravity on the Moon?

Why does the Moon change shape each night?

Is there any weather on the Moon?

Guess what?
The harder you look, and the more questions you ask, the more interested you become.

By asking yourself questions as you learn, *"the first Moon landing"* changes from something you need to know for your homework into something that's really interesting. Once you start asking yourself questions, you'll begin to wonder and explore, and that's what learning is all about!

EARTHQUAKES
Why do earthquakes happen?
Where do they happen?
What is an epicenter?
What is a fault?
How do you measure them?

Jot them down

You don't have to ask the questions out loud—you can make them up in your head. But it's a good idea to jot them down on separate pieces of paper—and check them off when you've found the answer.

When you ask questions, your brain automatically goes into search mode, on the look-out for the answers. So having a list of questions in front of you helps you to listen better and it improves your concentration.

Because they are your questions they are important to you. So you are much more likely to remember the answers!

Remember: all knowledge is just the answer to a question!

What? When? Why? How? Where? Who?

Constant questioning is the first key to wisdom!

"Six honest serving men"

Look back at the questions about the first landing on the Moon—those in bold. *Can you remember them?*

Now look at this. It might help!
"I keep six honest serving men,
They taught me all I knew,
*Their names are **What** and **Why** and **When**,*
*And **How** and **Where** and **Who**."*

It's a saying by a famous children's author called Rudyard Kipling! Learn it by heart and repeat it to yourself whenever you ask yourself questions.

Coach's Hot Tip

If you're reading a book, just take the main headings and turn them into questions.

Your 3 learning senses

It's not difficult to see that with 100 billion brain cells, everyone has the ability to become a learning CHAMP. But how do you actually use your brain to learn?

First you have to get the information you're learning *into* your brain—through one or more of your learning senses. So you'll either be *seeing* it, *hearing* it, or getting *physically* involved with it (doing something as you learn).

Remember! You'll get a chance to find out your favorite ways to take in information later in the book.

Then you have to *think* about that information to make sense of it. Otherwise, it goes in one ear and out the other! The fact that everyone has a favorite way of taking in information is a big reason why people learn in different ways.

HOW DO YOU LIKE TO LEARN?

1. By hearing things—like listening to your teacher, stories, or audio-tapes? Then you're more of an **audio** (or auditory) learner.

2. By seeing things—like posters, pictures, videos, computers, or the TV? Then you're more of a **visual** learner.

3. By writing notes, moving around as you learn, making models, or acting things out? Then you're more of a **physical** learner.

Easy peasy Japanesy!

What if you used all your senses as you learn? Would that make it easier? Here's a chance to try—by learning how to count from 1-10 in Japanese in just a few minutes.

Read the Japanese word for each number to yourself. Now say each word out loud (they are pronounced just as they look) as you act out the action.

ENGLISH	JAPANESE	WHAT YOU DO
One	itchi	scratch your knee and say 'itchy knee'
Two	ni	(that's 1 & 2)
Three	san	then say "sun, she go rock" as you point to the sun
Four	shi	point to a girl
Five	go	walk forward
Six	roco	then shake your hips in a rock and roll action (that's 3, 4, 5, and 6)
Seven	shichi	now do two sneezes, "shi chi" (that's 7)
Eight	hachi	pretend to put a hat on while you say "hatchi" (that's 8)
Nine	kyu	then "coo" like a dove from above (that's 9)
Ten	ju	think of "ju" the first syllable in Jupiter (that's 10)

Now do the exercise 2 more times.

You learned so quickly because you *read* the words, you *listened*, and you *acted* it out. You used your three learning senses together —and it was fun. And, guess what, that means you'll remember it much more easily too!

Coach's Hot Tip

The more you can see it, hear it, say it, and do it, the easier it is to learn!

Using your senses

Learning CHAMPS use all their senses to learn. They're called multi-sensory learners because they *V.A.P.* it. That means they use their *visual*, *auditory*, and *physical* senses all together! Here's how you can learn to *V.A.P.* it too!

VISUAL + **AUDITORY** + **PHYSICAL** = **MULTI SENSORY LEARNER** = **LEARNING CHAMP**

DID YOU KNOW?

Most people remember:

20% of what they **READ!**

30% of what they **HEAR!**

40% of what they **SEE!**

50% of what they **SAY!**

60% of what they **DO!**

But, if they **read**, **hear**, **see**, **say**, and **do** something with that information, they remember **90%** of it!

It makes sense!

The secret is to do something *extra* while you read or listen in order to make what you are learning stick in your mind.

When you become a more active learner and *look*, *listen*, and *do*, you use more of your brain cells and make many more connections between them!

You know what happens then, don't you? That's right! The more connections you make between your brain cells, the *cleverer* you become!

Look back at that table!

- Reading, by itself, is not enough. You only remember *20%* of what you *read*.
- Listening, by itself, is not enough. You only remember about *30%* of what you *hear*. Yet most school work is reading and listening!

Did you know? Multi-sensory learners use three different parts of their brain instead of just one!

Get the facts: visually

About 60 percent of your whole brain is involved in making sense of what you see. That's because you see things all the time except, of course, when you're asleep! It explains why people like pictures and television so much. It also makes sense of the expression: "*A picture is worth a thousand words*".

Visual people are often neat and tidy and like to look good. They tend to like detail, prefer well illustrated books to lectures, are often good at drawing, and may daydream, scribble, or doodle. But, whatever you prefer, it's wise to use some visual techniques, like these, as you learn.

Coach's Hot Tip

Highlighting really works because you mark for yourself what you DIDN'T already know.

Highlighting

Use a highlighter pen to highlight any important bits of *new* information.

Only highlight information that's new to you. Most learners make the mistake of highlighting everything on a page that they think is important.

If you highlight everything it only takes longer to read the text when you come back to revise at a later date. All you need are the new or difficult bits of information.

Try using different colored pens for different types of information.

Learning maps

Learning maps are a brilliant way to help you remember important things. In fact they are one of the very *best* learning techniques of all. Have a look at the learning map on page 36. It reminds you of all the things you learned in Step 1 of CHAMPS.

You can use learning maps for lots of things like:
• mapping out what you already know
• revision
• understanding the connections between ideas
• brainstorming new ideas
• planning—stories and project work

THINGS TO REMEMBER ABOUT LEARNING MAPS:

1. Always use blank paper.

2. Use it portrait or landscape.

3. Begin in the center.

4. Draw a colorful picture in the middle to show the topic, or write the title in **bold** in the middle.

5. Only use the **key** words you want to remember. This is the most important rule.

6. Write the main topics of the subject on thick "branches".

7. Put sub-topics and details on smaller, thinner "branches".

8. Print one word on a line in **bold** CAPITAL letters—these are your **key** words.

9. Organize your map—you may want to group some ideas together, or draw lines or arrows to connect things.

10. Put question marks on things you don't understand or would like to come back to later.

11. Use as much color and as many symbols and pictures as you can.

12. Don't crowd the page—leave lots of white space.

13. Really use your imagination.

14. Enjoy it!

Coach's Hot Tip

Don't worry if you have to redraw your map. It's a good way of helping it stick in your long-term memory.

Remember!

The emotional part of your brain likes color, so using different colors will help you learn.

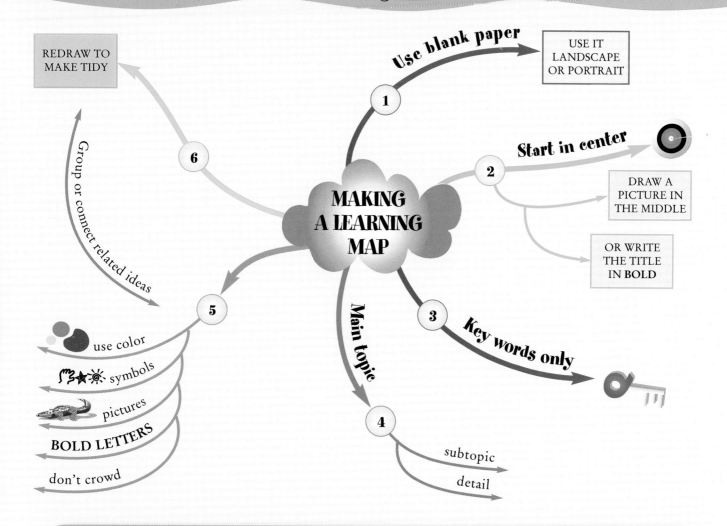

REDRAW TO MAKE TIDY

Use blank paper

USE IT LANDSCAPE OR PORTRAIT

Group or connect related ideas

6

MAKING A LEARNING MAP

Start in center

2

DRAW A PICTURE IN THE MIDDLE

OR WRITE THE TITLE IN **BOLD**

5

Main topic

3

Key words only

use color

symbols

pictures

BOLD LETTERS

don't crowd

4

subtopic

detail

WHY LEARNING MAPS ARE A NUMBER 1 LEARNING TECHNIQUE:

1. When information is presented in this way it's very easy to remember.

2. Remember—"a picture is worth a thousand words"!

3. Your brain prefers pictures and colors to words that are black and white.

4. You can see the "big picture" and the details that make up that picture at the same time.

5. You can see which are the most important things, because they are closer to the center.

6. All the branches that have the same color have information about one topic.

7. They help you to think more deeply about what you are learning.

8. You use all your learning senses together.

9. You will enjoy doing it so you are much more likely to remember it!

Get the facts: visually

Mental movies

Try making a "mental movie" (a movie in your head) of what you are learning. Picture in your mind what you have just seen, read, or heard. Mental movies help you store the information in your visual memory.

Pictures and posters

Drawing your own colorful pictures or posters are a brilliant way to record things like the parts of the body, how the heart works in biology, or how volcanoes happen. Use different colors to show how different groups connect with each other.

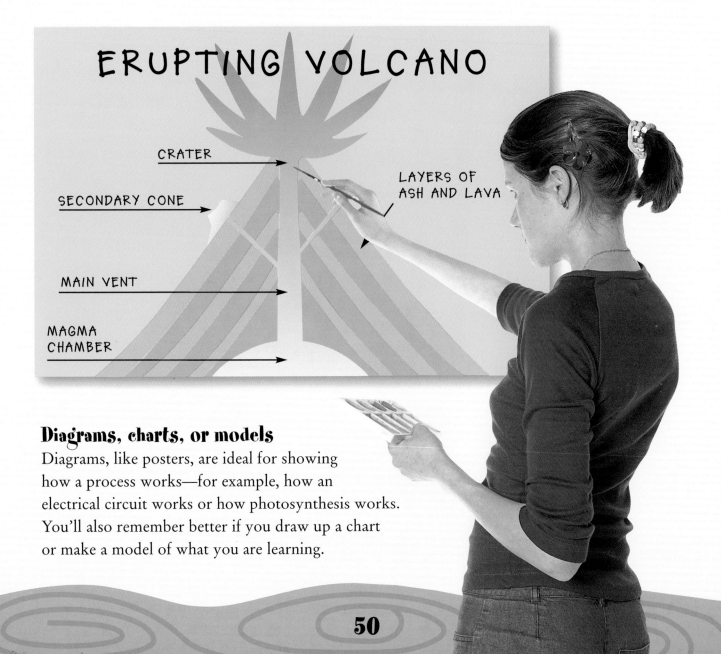

ERUPTING VOLCANO

CRATER

SECONDARY CONE

LAYERS OF
ASH AND LAVA

MAIN VENT

MAGMA
CHAMBER

Diagrams, charts, or models

Diagrams, like posters, are ideal for showing how a process works—for example, how an electrical circuit works or how photosynthesis works. You'll also remember better if you draw up a chart or make a model of what you are learning.

50

Get the facts: on audio!

Auditory people like to talk to themselves, sing aloud, and give speeches. They are good at telling jokes, they listen well, speak well, enjoy chatting and discussing things, and prefer to be given instructions verbally. Here are some great audio learning techniques.

Read it dramatically

Most people remember things that are dramatic. So if you find a bit of text in a book that's a little difficult, read it out loud, dramatically.

You could have a go at whispering it—or reading it in a foreign accent. Because it's unusual, you're bound to remember it.

Make a tape

Record the key points of what you are learning on a tape recorder. The effort will help lock all those facts away in your memory and you can revise as you go along in a bus or car.

Teach a friend

Give a friend or one of your parents a short account, in your own words, of what you are learning. The sound of your voice helps you to remember the facts.

Coach's Hot Tip

Try shouting out math or science formulas from one side of the room to the other with a friend!

Get the facts: physically

Many physical people like to move around a lot, write things down, like action words, sports and games. They enjoy making things, and often fidget or use their hands as they speak. They also find that they can remember places better if they visit them. These techniques will help you become a physical learner.

Powerful postcards

Write down the important things about a subject on postcards or "post-it" notes. That's because postcards are so small and you can only write a few key words on them. These words will jump out at you when you look back at them.

Stick all the cards or "post-it" notes on a big sheet of paper. This lets you *physically* sort out your thoughts on the subject.

Make a model

If possible, make a model of what you are learning out of paper, cardboard, or modelling clay. It's a useful technique for learning lots of facts in physics and chemistry.

Move it!

Try walking about as you learn, or, at least, get up and move every 25-30 minutes.

Act it out!

Acting out what you are learning won't fail to help you remember! You can act out lots of things—pretending to be an historical character or, with some friends, how parts of an atom fit together. It becomes *very* memorable.

Check it off

Get into the habit of checking off each idea when you have really understood it. Then you can see exactly where you started to get lost—just after the last check!

Studdy buddy

Learn with a friend so you can brainstorm ideas together and ask each other questions.

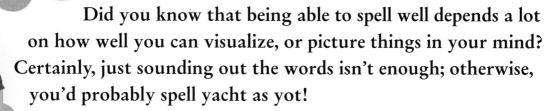

Yacht

Did you know that being able to spell well depends a lot on how well you can visualize, or picture things in your mind? Certainly, just sounding out the words isn't enough; otherwise, you'd probably spell yacht as yot!

Here's a technique that will improve your spelling straight away—it uses all your senses!

Now imagine (or visualize) all four syllables as if they were written on a board in white chalk. Imagine the board is slightly above your eye level.

How do you spell psychiatrist?

First divide the word into syllables. For example, the word psychiatrist (someone who deals with mental problems) would be split up like this:
PSY - CHI - A - TRIST

Close your eyes and repeat the individual letters and then the sound of the syllables. Try to see the letters as clearly as you can.

Next say the individual letters of the first syllable out-loud —**P-S-Y**. Then say the whole syllable, which is pronounced **SY**.

PSY-CHI-A-TRIST

Finally write the word down in **bold** letters and maybe in different colors while you spell it out as a whole word and say it out loud as a whole word.

Now spell out the second syllable —**C-H-I.** Then pronounce the second syllable like this—**KI**.

Then the third syllable—**A**.

Now you've **seen** the word, you've **heard** it, you've **written** it and, most importantly, you've broken it down visually.

Finally spell out the fourth syllable—**T-R-I-S-T** and pronounce it like this —**TRIST**.

**Guess what?
I bet you'll never forget how to spell the word "psychiatrist"!**

PSY-CHI-A-TRIST
PSY-CHI-A-TRIST
PSY-CHI-A-TRIST

Listening skills

It may surprise you, but being a good listener is a real skill. Most people only listen in spurts and can think at least four times faster than anyone can talk! So it's easy to lose your concentration. But if you listen properly the first time, you'll save yourself a lot of time later on. Here's how you can teach yourself to become a champion listener!

You always hear, but maybe you don't always listen!

The better you listen, the smarter you'll be.

Warm up first

What did you cover in your last lesson? Remember for a minute, then check your notes. It's *much* easier to learn new stuff if you can *link* it to what you already know.

On your way to your next lesson, get into the right frame of mind by imagining what you'll be studying. Be on time for your class, sit up front, join in, and always try to show interest.

Imagine it's just for you

Imagine your teacher is talking to you personally. This helps you concentrate better. You wouldn't drift off during a one-to-one conversation, would you?

Keep those questions coming!

Remember how asking yourself questions is the secret to being interested and staying alert as you learn. It's just the same in class.

Keep asking yourself questions like:
- *"What's the main idea here?"*
- *"Could I put that in another way?"*
- *"What does he mean?"*

Listen for clues!

Your teacher has a *"lesson plan"*. It includes the two or three points that he or she will cover in the lesson. In your next lesson, listen and see if you can spot them!

When your teacher comes to a particularly important point, he or she may stress it in different ways.

He or she may:
- Simply say, *"These are the key points"*.
- Change her tone of voice.
- Get really excited.
- Write some *key* words or draw a diagram on the board (these are worth copying).

Make notes

Making notes is the best way to keep concentrating. It's a good idea to make a note of what you don't understand too. Jot down a *key* word to remind you and, if you get a chance, ask your teacher to explain it to you.

IMMUNE SYSTEM
What are antibodies?
Do white blood cells kill germs?
Why do we have red blood cells?
What is plasma?

Teachers prefer students who tell them when they don't understand something, to those who pretend to know everything, but don't really!

Reading skills

Do you remember that when you first learned to read, you used a finger or a piece of card to help you to *"keep your place"* on the page? You can use this same technique to help you become a better reader and to speed up your reading now that you're older. Follow these five important steps to help you become an even speedier reader.

Guess what?

Using your finger as a guide helps your eyes go smoothly along the line of words.

3. Next you read . . .

Now read through the text, looking out for the main ideas, and jotting down any topics you find difficult or don't understand.

1. First you scan . . .

Scan the chapter headings and the section headings. Then scan the illustrations and diagrams—they'll give you a feel (the *"big picture"*) of what it's all about.

4. . . . as you make notes!

Always read a textbook with a pencil in your hand! Then you can make notes as you go. You can jot them down as a *learning map*, or on postcards, or "post-it" notes or, in fact, any style that suits you.

2. Then you question . . .

Ask yourself these two questions:
- *"What do I already know?"* (Jot down the *key* words.)
- *"What are the main new ideas that I need to know more about?"* (You'll know what they are from doing the scan!)

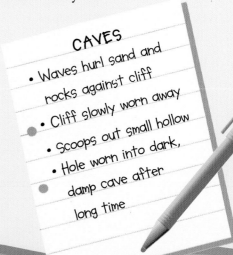

CAVES
- Waves hurl sand and rocks against cliff
- Cliff slowly worn away
- Scoops out small hollow
- Hole worn into dark, damp cave after long time

But remember to only use *key* words—the words that, when you read them again, will remind you of the main ideas.

5. Finally you review

Finally sit back and tell yourself what you have learned. Go over your notes the next day to really lock it all away in your memory.

Reading like this is active reading. It saves time because you'll remember much more the first time—so you won't have to keep re-reading it later.

Become a super surfer

Do you need to find out about a famous person or invention? Are you learning about the universe? Do you need a picture to add to your homework or school project? If the answer is "*yes,*" then the Internet's for you. It's a great way to find out things on almost any subject you can possibly think of! And it's really handy if you have a lot of homework to do!

URLs

Every site on the web has it's own URL—which is short for *Uniform Resource Locator*. But sometimes all you have is the subject for the information you want. So here's what you do! You use a *search engine*.

Search engines

The home page of your *Internet Service Provider* (ISP) will have a button marked search. That's where you type in the subject you want to know about. But there are billions of web pages out there. So how do you get the page you want?

More about Mars

Say you wanted to find out about the weather on the planet Mars. If you type in weather you'll get thousands of sites about the weather.

If you just type in mars, you'll get information on Mars, the Roman god of war, Mars bars, biker mice from Mars, towns called Mars, and all sorts of stuff you don't need.

The answer is to go to one of the main search engines, like *Alta Vista*, or *Yahoo*—they'll let you do a much more sophisticated and detailed search.

Spiderman!

The best way to search for the weather on Mars is to type in planet+mars+weather. Then the search engine will send off a robot, called a *"spider,"* to find the pages that most nearly match your request— ignoring much of the irrelevant stuff.

You could even tell the search engine what not to look for. So you could type planet+mars-god.

SUPER SURFING RULES

1. Always ask one of your parents before you use the Internet. That's because there are lots of people out there you can't trust and there's some unsuitable material.

2. Use more than one search engine or directory.

3. If you save a picture from a web-site on the Net, it belongs to someone else. So, if you use it for a project, you need to type the person's name or where you got it from under that picture.

4. Make sure that any facts you get are from a reliable source, such as a university, or a government site, or organization like NASA. A great place to start is **teachernet**—this is a brilliant collection of school websites on all the main subjects at school.

5. Don't copy long chunks of text. The web is great for finding out lots of information—it's not there to stop you thinking for yourself!!

Learning map

Scan

Question

Read

Reading

Make notes

Review

8 skills

Super surfer

Search engines

Surfing rules

9

What's the big idea?

1

Get the big picture

Scan it

Take it step-by-step

What do I already know?

Connect to last lesson

Listening

7 skills

Ask questions

Listen for clues

Make notes

Sit up front

Step 2
HOME IN ON
THE FACTS

Ask questions

2

When? How? Where? Who? What? Why?

Visualize each syllable

6

PSY-CHI-A-TRIST

Super spellers

physically

Get the facts

5

Study buddies

Act it out

Make a model

Check it off

Get the facts on audio

4

Make a tape

Teach a friend

Read it dramatically

Get the facts

3

Highlight

Learning maps

Mental movies

Pictures and posters

Diagrams

Step 3

ACTION!

Unless you try, you don't know what you can't do!

Introduction

There's a big difference between knowing about
something and really understanding it.

Remember in Step 2 you discovered how to use
your senses (your eyes, your ears, and your body)
to get new information into your brain?

Well, in Step 3 (which is probably the most important step of all)
you're going to learn how to take the right action to help you
THINK ABOUT and UNDERSTAND that new information.

And you're going to do something to it so that you change
it from someone else's ideas into your own.

You only learn when you think!

Think about this! An acre is a measure of land. It's about 13,560 square feet. That's information. It's easy to forget because it's just a boring old number which doesn't mean much. But if you were to explore it and think a bit deeper you would discover that an acre is also about the size of a soccer field.

13,560 square feet?

Now you *understand* an acre—because you've seen a soccer field and you can picture it in your head.

You've changed what was just information and easy to forget into something you understand and can remember. In this case by *thinking* with your *visual* intelligence.

The only way to learn something properly is to stop and *think* about it. So we're going to show you some brilliant techniques that'll help you *think* and *remember* whatever you want.

While you're thinking, you're learning!

Your 8 intelligences

Once you have taken in new information through your senses, you have to use your intelligences to think about that information. Did you notice the *s* on the end of intelligences? That's because people don't only have one kind of intelligence, or even two. They actually have 8. That means they have 8 different ways of thinking!

It's not a question of "How smart are you?" It's a question of "How are you smart?"

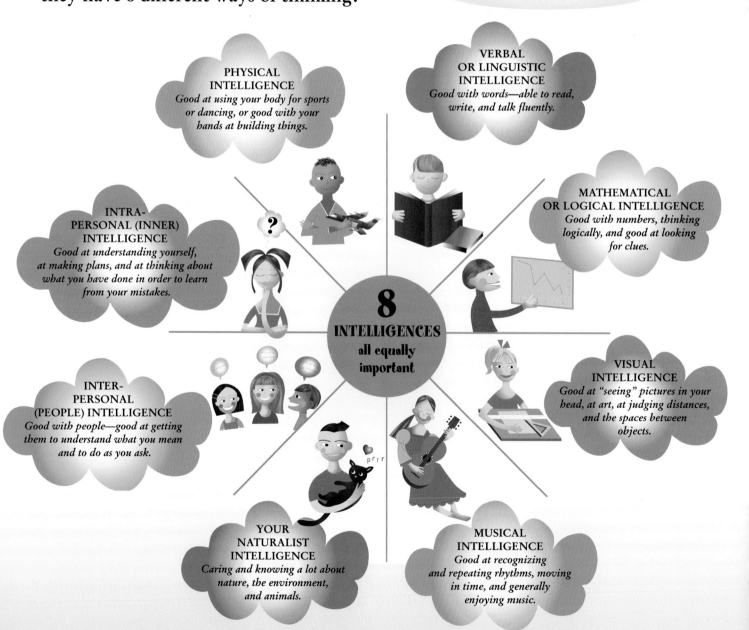

PHYSICAL INTELLIGENCE
Good at using your body for sports or dancing, or good with your hands at building things.

VERBAL OR LINGUISTIC INTELLIGENCE
Good with words—able to read, write, and talk fluently.

INTRA-PERSONAL (INNER) INTELLIGENCE
Good at understanding yourself, at making plans, and at thinking about what you have done in order to learn from your mistakes.

MATHEMATICAL OR LOGICAL INTELLIGENCE
Good with numbers, thinking logically, and good at looking for clues.

8 INTELLIGENCES all equally important

INTER-PERSONAL (PEOPLE) INTELLIGENCE
Good with people—good at getting them to understand what you mean and to do as you ask.

VISUAL INTELLIGENCE
Good at "seeing" pictures in your head, at art, at judging distances, and the spaces between objects.

YOUR NATURALIST INTELLIGENCE
Caring and knowing a lot about nature, the environment, and animals.

MUSICAL INTELLIGENCE
Good at recognizing and repeating rhythms, moving in time, and generally enjoying music.

Your 8 intelligences

Which are your strongest intelligences?

Which of these statements apply to you most? You will find that you agree with more statements for some intelligences than others. They will tend to be your strongest intelligences.

Then read the techniques on pages 66–72 and decide which of them will best suit the way you like to learn. You can use them to make learning easier and more successful.

LINGUISTIC

I enjoy reading books, plays, and poetry.
I find it easy to learn from books, tapes, the Internet, and lectures.
I'm a good talker.
I'm good at writing stories.
I enjoy crossword puzzles and word games.

MATHEMATICAL/LOGICAL

I like to solve puzzles and problems.
I like science and learn well through logical explanations.
I'm good at estimating and measuring.
I approach tasks in a logical step-by-step way.
I'm good at mental arithmetic and working out numbers.

VISUAL/SPATIAL

I have a good sense of direction.
I'm good at picturing things "in my mind's eye" (visualizing).
I'm good at judging distances.
I learn well from charts, diagrams, and maps.
I'm good at art, modelling, or sculpture.

MUSICAL

I remember verse/poetry/jingles well.
I enjoy listening to music.
I can recognize tunes easily.
I have a good sense of rhythm.
I enjoy the sounds of nature.
I'm good at singing, or playing an instrument.

INTER-PERSONAL

I learn well and like to work in a group or team.
I'm good at getting others to go along with my ideas.
I make friends easily.
I can help with problems between other people.

INTRA-PERSONAL

I enjoy working/learning quietly on my own.
I like to day-dream, imagine and fantasize.
I'm good at forming my own opinions.
I keep a personal diary or journal.
I'm good at making plans and setting goals for myself.
I'm good at learning from my mistakes and experience.

PHYSICAL

I'm good at sports and games.
I like dancing and physical exercise.
I'm good at "hands-on" learning.
I'm skillful when working with things.
I like to deal with physical problems.
I'm good at building things.

NATURALIST

I keep a pet and/or I like animals.
I can recognize and name quite a few plants, trees, and flowers.
I can read weather signs and wildlife tracks, and I feel close to nature.
I'm concerned about the environment and pollution.

Using your verbal intelligence

Put it in your own words

Putting something into your own words is a brilliant way of making sure you really have understood it. All you have to do is put down the textbook you're learning from and jot down from memory all the main things you feel are important. Then go back and have a look at the textbook for any important ideas you may have missed out.

• Egyptians believed that the dead • traveled to another world

You can use the same idea when you're reading. Simply put down your book at the end of each main section or chapter and jot down the *key* ideas in your own words. Saying these main points out loud will help you remember.

Flash cards

Creating your own flash cards with just the *key* words or *bullet points* of the topic works really well for most subjects. They are helpful when you need to revise what you know later.

Answer your own questions

Always remember to ask questions as you read and listen. Then try to answer the questions yourself.

ANCIENT EGYPT—MUMMIES

- Body dried out for 40 days in natron
- Rubbed in ointments
- Wrapped in bandages
- Coffin put in stone case (sarcophagus)

Next you need to organize these notes in a logical way. You could make a *learning map* (see pages 48-49) or jot them down on index cards that you can put in order later on.

If you're not asking questions, you're probably not learning.

• took out brain through nose • kept heart

• Ointments • Bandages • Sarcophagus

Using your mathematical intelligence

Put things in order

When you have read or heard about a new subject, choose what you think are the most important points, and jot down the *key* words. Then put these points in the order you think is the most important.

THE EARTH'S CRUST

1. Crust (rocky layer)
2. Mantle (thick layer of hot rock)
3. Outer core (liquid metal)
4. Inner core (solid metal) (9,032°F at center of earth)

It's a good way to learn because when you put things in order, you compare them with each other. That means you have to *think* about them more deeply. And, as you already know, while your *thinking*, you're *learning*!

Analyse it!

Asking yourself questions as you learn means you're not just reading or listening—you're analyzing the subject, which is just another way of saying you're thinking about the words more deeply.

These are the kinds of questions you could ask yourself:

- What is the main point?
- Can I think of a better example for this?
  - What conclusions come from this idea?
  - What's the evidence?
  - If this is true what else must be true?
- How can I use this?
- Is this a fact that can be proved—or just someone's opinion?

Sort 'em out

Sometimes you can break a subject down into groups. If you can, see if you can sort the main points of what you're learning into, say, three different groups, like this.

ADJECTIVE	VERB	NOUN
fierce	fly	ladder
frightened	burn	table
furry	shop	chimpanzee
large	collect	daffodil
pretty	chase	rocket
beautiful	polish	bottle

Predict it!

When you're reading or listening, try to predict what is going to happen next. It keeps you alert and when the answer comes it's easier to remember because you can match up your prediction with the actual answer.

Using your visual intelligence

Learning maps

Remember you found out how *learning maps* are a brilliant visual way to get the key facts as you learn (see pages 48-49). They're a great way to think about what you're learning too! It often helps to redraw a learning map in a more logical way. Perhaps you want to add subheads, symbols, or color coding to each main branch.

Diagrams and posters

Often the best way to solve a problem or see how things connect together is to draw a diagram, like the one of a tooth below. Sometimes a poster works better, say for parts of the body in biology, or for learning French words.

Be a TV reporter

Many school topics are fun to visualize as a sort of "mental TV documentary".

Suppose you were learning about an event in history—say the development of the Roman Empire—you could plan an imaginary film about it. Imagine you have a multi-million dollar budget to spend, your favorite film stars, an exotic location, a cast of thousands, as well as spectacular special effects! *How would it begin? How would it progress? How would it end?* After all it's only in your mind!

But it really **will** help you remember all about the Roman Empire!

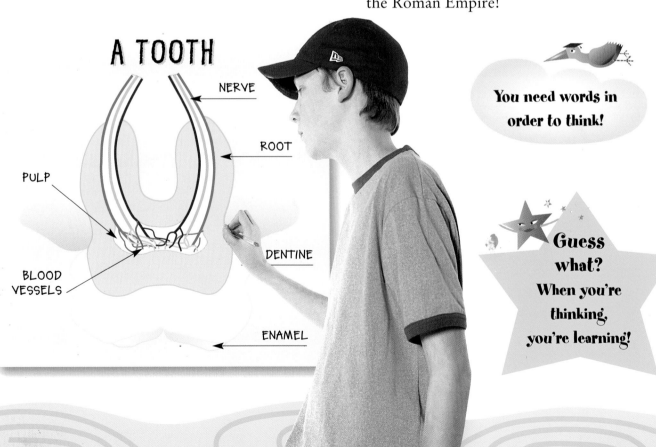

A TOOTH

NERVE

ROOT

PULP

DENTINE

BLOOD VESSELS

ENAMEL

You need words in order to think!

Guess what? When you're thinking, you're learning!

Using your musical intelligence

Rap it up!

You probably know the words to lots of songs! And you probably never even tried to learn them!

Words with music are easy to learn. That's because adding some rhythm and rhyme makes it easier to remember. And that's why so many advertisements have catchy jingles! Try chanting math or science rules or historical dates to music.

Coach's Hot Tip

Try making up a rhyme, rap, or song about what you're learning. It works because you really have to think about what you're learning to fit the words to a tune.

In 14 hundred and 92 Columbus sailed the ocean blue

Background music

The emotional center of your brain gets really excited by music. That's the part that's responsible for your memory too. For some people, the right background music helps to make them more alert and to concentrate better. Especially if it's something without words that's not too loud!

You could also have a go at learning songs in a foreign language – it's a great way to increase your vocabulary!

It's also true that the music of some composers like Mozart, Haydn, and Handel may help you learn. So why not experiment with some quiet classical music in the background as you do your homework!

Using your physical intelligence

Don't forget to write it down!

Write it down

Remember that writing is a *physical* exercise. So when you write notes you add *physical* (writing) to *visual* (the words) to *audio* (the sound you make if you say the words out loud).

Then, guess what, you've *V.A.Ped* it—that means you've used your *visual, auditory,* and *physical* senses all together (see page 46). That's why written notes make things easier to learn.

Act it out

It really helps to act out the words when you are learning a foreign language. That's because it's not just your mind that stores memories, your body does too!

If you say, *"Je suis triste"* ("*I am sad*" in French) out loud while you make a sad face and hunch your shoulders, you add a physical memory to the sound of your voice and the written words.

Thoughtful index cards

Put the main points of what you are learning on plain index cards or "post-it" notes—just one main idea on each card. Then sort them out on a table into a logical order.

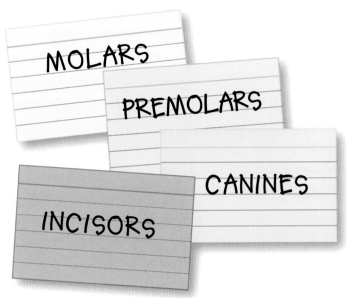

MOLARS
PREMOLARS
CANINES
INCISORS

You're now taking thoughts, which are pretty slippery things, and making them into things you can move and touch.

Later on, you can add detail to these index cards and turn them into revision cards (see page 82).

"Je suis triste"

Using your inter-personal intelligence

Teach it

There's a saying that goes, "*The best way to learn is to teach*". It's true! That's because when you teach something to someone else, you have to organize your thoughts and put them into your own words.

It's easy to think you understand something, but when you have to explain it out loud, it forces you to clear up any unclear thoughts. So try explaining what you've learned to a friend or one of your parents.

Study buddies

Study buddies make learning more fun and easier to remember—doing things on your own is never so interesting. And you begin to learn how to work with other people. That's an important skill you'll need when you get a job one day.

So you could, for example, each learn half of a homework topic and then teach each other what you have learned. Then you can write it down—as individuals, of course!

Compare notes

At the end of a project or book, compare your notes with a friend or study buddy. You'll be surprised at the things they remembered that you didn't and the other way round.

Two heads are better than one!

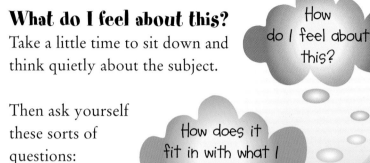

What do I feel about this?

Take a little time to sit down and think quietly about the subject.

Then ask yourself these sorts of questions:

How do I feel about this?

How might this be important to me?

How does it fit in with what I already know?

Can this benefit me in any way?

What would it be like to be one of the characters I'm learning about?

What will I get out of learning this?

Compare it

Another good way to understand something is to compare the new idea with something you already know. Say, you were learning about the first Moon landing, you could compare it to other first long journeys in history, such as Columbus' or Magellan's. Compare the training each person had, the preparation for each journey, and the amount of time it took.

The human touch

It's true that when you're interested you learn well—you don't have to be nagged to learn a hobby you like or a computer game, do you?

So if you have a subject that seems a bit boring to you, look for the human interest—some facts about the people involved.

- *Who first invented this?*
- *What were they like?*
- *What happened to them?*

Putting it all together

You've probably spotted that there are no activities for using your *Naturalist Intelligence*. That's because, although it's important, it's not so easy to **think** or learn with it. So it's better to use it as a way of checking whether what you're learning about will affect the environment—or other people.

You've found out that most people are stronger in some of their intelligences than others. So they find some tasks easier to do than others.

But they are all as important as each other. It's just that each person is intelligent in different ways.

So it makes sense to start by using your strongest intelligence as you learn.

You've found out all kinds of different ways to think and learn. *Which ones will you use for your school work? Which lesson are you going to start with?*

You wouldn't use more than one or two techniques for any one subject. That's because different types of subjects need different types of learning techniques.

Now think about this!

The more of your *intelligences* you develop, the more *brainpower* you use.

The more *brainpower* you create, the more *thinking* you do.

The more *thinking* you do, the more *connections* you make in your brain.

And, the more *connections* you make, the *cleverer* you become.

It's as simple as that!

Learning map

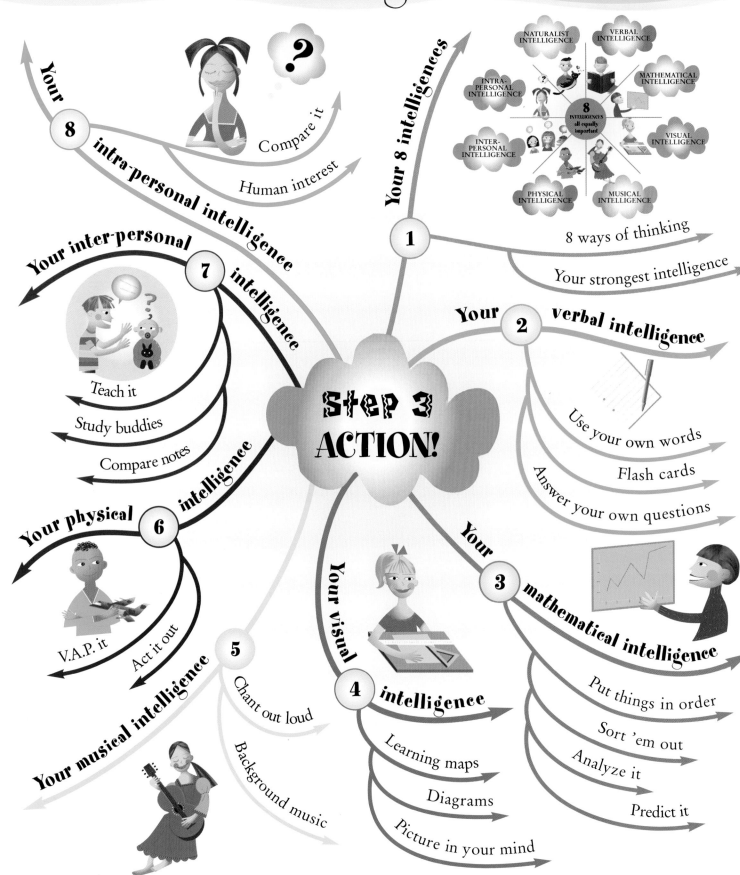

Step 3 ACTION!

1 — Your 8 intelligences
- NATURALIST INTELLIGENCE
- VERBAL INTELLIGENCE
- MATHEMATICAL INTELLIGENCE
- VISUAL INTELLIGENCE
- MUSICAL INTELLIGENCE
- PHYSICAL INTELLIGENCE
- INTER-PERSONAL INTELLIGENCE
- INTRA-PERSONAL INTELLIGENCE
- 8 INTELLIGENCES all equally important
- 8 ways of thinking
- Your strongest intelligence

2 — Your verbal intelligence
- Use your own words
- Flash cards
- Answer your own questions

3 — Your mathematical intelligence
- Put things in order
- Sort 'em out
- Analyze it
- Predict it

4 — Your visual intelligence
- Learning maps
- Diagrams
- Picture in your mind

5 — Your musical intelligence
- Chant out loud
- Background music

6 — Your physical intelligence
- V.A.P. it
- Act it out

7 — Your inter-personal intelligence
- Teach it
- Study buddies
- Compare notes

8 — Your intra-personal intelligence
- Compare it
- Human interest

Step 4
MEMORIZE IT!

Everything you learn depends on your memory. Without it, you'd have to keep learning things over and over again.

Introduction

Right, so you've found out how to take in information and use all your intelligences to think about it more deeply. Now you need to remember that information so you can use it again.

Step 4 of CHAMPS will show you how your memory works best and it will teach you all kinds of techniques that will help you to develop a really super memory. That's a big step to becoming a learning CHAMP!

How your memory works

It's hard to believe but within 24 hours you'll have forgotten almost three-quarters of what you learned today *unless* you make a special effort to remember it! Luckily, there are lots of ways to help you remember things more easily. But first it helps to know how your memory works.

You already have a great memory!

You really *do* already have a great memory. Here's how you can test it!

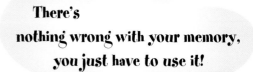

There's nothing wrong with your memory, you just have to use it!

Imagine your bedroom. Start at the door and gradually look around it—in your mind's eye. *Can you remember where the bed is*? Picture the furniture and the windows. *What color are the drapes and carpet? Do you "see" any toys or books there?*

Did you know? Most people naturally look upward to the left when they are remembering something. (But not everybody!)

Now remember your bedroom again. But this time notice where your eyes are looking. Are they looking up, or down, or even sideways?

You will often find that you recall things more easily if you look in the same direction that your eyes look naturally. *Try it—it works.*

Short- and long-term memory

You have two types of memory—your short-term memory and your long-term memory.

"Shichi!!!"

Your short-term memory can only hold about seven pieces of  information at once—things like repeating a new name or writing down a math answer you just worked on. Your long-term memory is more like a permanent filing cabinet.

To switch something from your short- to your long-term memory you need to **do** something with that information.

Remember *Easy peasy Japanesy* (see page 45)? You **looked** at the words, you **listened** to the way they sounded, you **said** them out loud, and you **did** something that was unusual and quite funny.

In other words you **V.A.Ped** it. You used your senses as you learned—so you stored the information in different parts of your brain.

YOU REMEMBER THINGS WHEN:

1. They're interesting or exciting to you.
2. You're relaxed and involve your emotions.
3. They're surprising, unusual, funny, or rude.
4. You understand them.
5. They're colorful.
6. They're at the beginning or end of a work session.
7. You say them out loud.

YOU FORGET THINGS WHEN:

1. You don't understand them properly.
2. You're tired, anxious, or stressed.
3. You don't listen or pay attention.
4. You try to remember too much at once.
5. You don't repeat things enough times.
6. You work for more than 30 minutes at a time.
7. You're distracted by other things.

Get physical

Most people are good at remembering physical experiences, like riding a bike, swimming, or going on an airplane. That's because when you do something physical as you learn, you don't forget it. It's the same when you act out what you are learning.

Say you were learning these French words, *sauter*, *rire*, and *chien* you could:
• *jump* into the air as you say *sauter* (to jump)
• *laugh* as you say *rire* (to laugh)
• *bark* as you say *chien* (dog)
You'll remember them much better if you do!

"Sauter!"

Picture it

Remember you found out earlier that 60 percent of your whole brain is involved in the process of seeing. So, if you can picture the information in your mind, you're much more likely to remember it.

For example—what's the easiest to remember—this list of all the countries in South America?

Or this map of the same countries?

Link it

It's much easier to learn new things if you can *link*, or **connect**, them to something you already know. That's how you learned when you were young.

Say you're learning colors in a foreign language. It's easier to learn the words as a group—blue, red, yellow, etc. That's because they're all associated with one another. So when you remember one, you tend to remember the others too.

Venezuela	Colombia	Guyana	Suriname
Uruguay	Ecuador	Peru	Brazil
Bolivia	Chile	Argentina	Paraguay
	French Guiana		

79

How your memory works

Repeat it

Do you remember that when you were small, you liked to hear the same story, watch the same video, or play the same game again and again? You did that because your brain likes to be sure of the information. It likes to go over it again and search out what it means.

To make sure information is switched from your short-term to long-term memory, you need to repeat it—about 4 times? That goes for reviewing things too! You don't have to go over all the text in full—just check the main points for a few minutes.

Divide it up!

Do you sometimes only remember the beginning and the end of a lesson and feel that the middle is a bit hazy? That's natural. Your brain finds it much easier to remember beginnings and endings. So don't have long study periods—have lots of short ones.

If you study for a long period, there is one beginning and one end. But if you divide that one long period up into 4 short ones, you have 4 beginnings and 4 endings. So you remember more.

Sleep on it!

You sleep to rest your body and recover your energy. You also sleep so your brain can make sense of what you've learned during the day.

While you sleep your eyes sometimes move around rapidly. During this time, called the period of *R.E.M.* sleep (*Rapid Eye Movement*), your brain is remembering what you learned during the day and filing it away for future use!

If you review your notes for about 5 minutes, half-an-hour before you go to sleep, it gives your brain something to work on. Check the main parts for a few minutes first thing in the morning and you'll really "lock it all down" in your memory.

Guess what?
Tests show that this pattern of learning can improve your memory of the topic by as much as 6 times!!!

Developing a super memory

Has your mom or dad ever forgotten where he or she left the car in a parking lot? Did they think they were losing their memory? Don't worry—they probably didn't know where it was in the first place! That's because they never really tried to remember—they probably had other things on their mind!

Pay attention!

The first step to a super memory is to *pay attention!* It's really easy—just say to yourself, "*I'm going to remember this!*" (If your mom or dad had really taken notice of the floor number of the parking lot and the space number he or she would have remembered it.)

Deciding to remember is one of the most important steps to developing a super memory!

Notice details

The next step is to notice the details of what you're learning. *Are there any colors, pictures, or unusual words on the page?* Think about the main new points you've learned. Then jot them down.

This means you're storing the information in more than one place in your brain.

Relax!

Remember—stress can make your mind go "*blank.*" So take a few deep breaths before you start to review (see page 24).

Developing a super memory

Revision cards

Remember you learned to put only the *key* points about the topic you're studying on flash cards (see page 66)? Well, these flash cards can now become *review cards*.

Review cards are brilliant because, as long as you have included all the *key* points, you no longer have to go back to your textbook. Just reading through them and remembering what the headings mean will be enough to remind you of all the detail.

You can use the cards to revise and test yourself—maybe when you're traveling or waiting for a bus (time that might otherwise be wasted). It's a simple, important idea that works because:

- Testing yourself is fun—like having a competition with yourself.
- The *key* words will trigger off the rest of the information in your mind.

Guess what? You could also record your review cards onto a tape or computer.

Here's how you might create some review cards for learning about disease and fighting disease.

BACTERIA (Microbes and germs)

1. About ONE THOUSAND TIMES smaller than a body cell.
2. Get energy from sunlight/chemicals and food.
3. Reproduce rapidly—divide every 20 minutes.
4. Cause illness by damaging cells and producing poisons—causes food to decay.
5. Vital in the digestive system. Used in sewage farms to "digest" waste.
6. Examples:
   Tooth decay—produces acid that attack teeth
   Bubonic plague, tuberculosis
   Ear infection

VIRUS (Microbes and germs)

1. Not cells—a tiny package of chemicals coated by protein.
2. About TEN THOUSAND TIMES smaller than a body cell.
3. Reproduce by invading body cells—then use the cells own chemicals to copy themselves.
4. Cause illness by damaging body cells.
5. Examples:
   Common cold, flu
   Chicken pox, mumps, measles
   Cold sores

FIVE WAYS MICROBES ENTER THE BODY

Where	How	Defence
Skin or eyes	Scratches/cuts	Blood clots seal the cut. Eyes produce chemical to kill bacteria
Digestive system	Contaminated food and dirty water	Hydrochloric acid in stomach kills bacteria.
Respiratory system	Microbes in the air enter nose and lungs	Mucus and tiny hairs in nose trap bacteria.
Animals	Mosquitos—suck blood Tsetsefly—sleeping sickness Rats, fleas—carry plague	No natural immunity—some immunization possible.

Flash maps

Review cards contain all the **key** points on a topic. But, you'll have quite a few topics over the course of a term. So, at the end of term, take just the title of all your review cards and make a *learning map* out of them.

Now you have a reminder of the whole course on one easy-to-memorize piece of paper.

Pole-bridging

Pole-bridging means doing a running commentary on what you're learning. Say you're performing a scientific experiment. When you pole-bridge, you describe exactly what you're doing, as you're doing it.

Now you have the sound of your own voice and your own words connected to the topic, so it's much easier to remember. That's because as you **read** and **talk** out loud at the same time, or **do** and **talk** at the same time, you are connecting up **both** sides of your brain.

Memory flashing

You've probably heard people saying, *"I wish I had a photographic memory!"* Well, it's easy to develop one. Here's how!

1. Check over the notes you've already made on the topic. (These could be bullet points, a learning map, a list, or a diagram.)

2. Put down the notes and see if you can recreate them correctly from memory.

3. When the new notes are the same as the original notes, you'll have stored them permanently in your brain.

Guess what? It really helps to look over your work and recreate it "in your head".

Now look at this diagram of an electrical circuit. Then cover it up and see if you can draw it without looking at it.

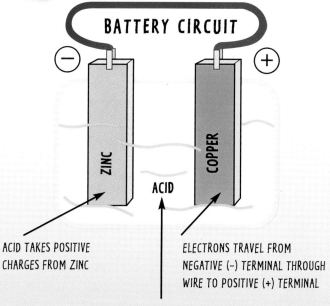

BATTERY CIRCUIT

ZINC

COPPER

ACID

ACID TAKES POSITIVE CHARGES FROM ZINC

ELECTRONS TRAVEL FROM NEGATIVE (−) TERMINAL THROUGH WIRE TO POSITIVE (+) TERMINAL

ACID TAKES ELECTRONS FROM COPPER

Numbered points

Another simple but useful memory technique is to number the points, ideas, or actions you need to remember. Then you'll automatically know if you've left something out!

Review it!

Do you remember that you need to repeat information about 4 times to make sure it's switched from your short-term to your long-term memory? And do you remember that you can lose up to 75 percent of what you read within 24 hours?

It's very important to review what you've learned in the days that follow (only for a very short time though—say 3 or 4 minutes). This helps it stick in your long-term memory. The best way to do this is to set up your own special review program.

Coach's Hot Tip

Only review the notes you took or the parts you highlighted. Go back to your textbook only if you want to get something clear.

THE IDEAL REVIEW PROGRAM:

1. Re-read your notes and test yourself on the key points.
2. Review them after an hour for about 5 minutes.
3. Review them again after one day for 3 minutes.
4. Review them again after one week for another 3 minutes.
5. Review them again after one month for about 2 minutes.
6. Review them again just before your exams for a few minutes.

Guess what?

A review program will improve your chances of remembering something by as much as four times—that's 400%!!!

After 6 months you should still remember 80-90% of the information. But without a review program you may only remember 20% of what you learn.

More terrific techniques

Do you remember that your brain prefers pictures to words? And that you can learn any new information if you "link" it to, or "associate" it with, something you already know and understand? Well, here are some terrific memory techniques that work because they use visualization and association.

They're often called "*mnemonics*" (*nem-on-ics*). A *mnemonic* is simply a way or "trick" to remember information.

Acronyms

An *acronym* is one of the most useful mnemonics. It's a word made up from the first letters of what you are trying to remember.

CHAMPS is an *acronym* for the 6 steps of this course! Here's how it works:

Coach's Hot Tip

Try making up your own acronyms as you learn. They'll help you to remember things forever after.

Here's an *acronym* for SCUBA (diving):

CHAMPS

C onfident to learn

H ome in on the facts

A ction!

M emorize it!

P rove you know

S it back and think

SCUBA

S elf

C ontained

U nderwater

B reathing

A pparatus

Creative sentences

My MERCURY

Very VENUS

Pole PLUTO

North NEPTUNE

Energetic EARTH

This is when you make up an interesting or funny story sentence to remind you of some important information. Here's one that'll help you to remember the planets in our solar system! Notice that the first letters of each word in the sentence are the same as the first letters of the words that you are trying to remember.

URANUS Under

MARS Mother

SATURN Swam

JUPITER Just

My	**M**ercury
Very	**V**enus
Energetic	**E**arth
Mother	**M**ars
Just	**J**upiter
Swam	**S**aturn
Under	**U**ranus
(the)	
North	**N**eptune
Pole	**P**luto

Coach's Hot Tip

Creative sentences work best when you can imagine what's happening in the sentence.

Here's a creative sentence that will help you remember the colors of the rainbow:

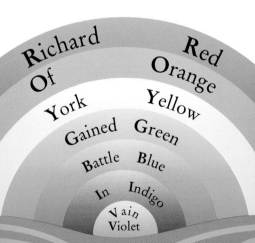

Richard Of York Gained Battle In Vain

Red Orange Yellow Green Blue Indigo Violet

Togetherwords

When you want to remember the name of something that needs to be linked to another piece of information—say that Rome is the capital of Italy—try running the names together.

So it would be:

- **Romeitaly**
- **Santiagochile**
- **Madridspain**
- **Lisbonportugal**

Remembering what you've forgotten!

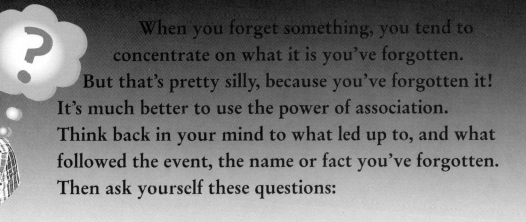

When you forget something, you tend to concentrate on what it is you've forgotten. But that's pretty silly, because you've forgotten it! It's much better to use the power of association. Think back in your mind to what led up to, and what followed the event, the name or fact you've forgotten. Then ask yourself these questions:

Who was I with?

What was I thinking, feeling, and saying?

Where was I at the time?

4,840 square yards equals one acre. I knew I'd remember in the end!

Think of it as a big hole into which the thing you've forgotten has disappeared.

When you have all the associations, say to yourself really positively "*I shall soon remember*". Now leave it to your subconscious, or inner mind, and you'll usually find that the answer will come racing back to you.

Coach's Hot Tip

If you forget someone's name or a place, go slowly through the alphabet. Then you'll probably get a strong feeling for which letter of the alphabet the forgotten name or place begins with.

Learning map

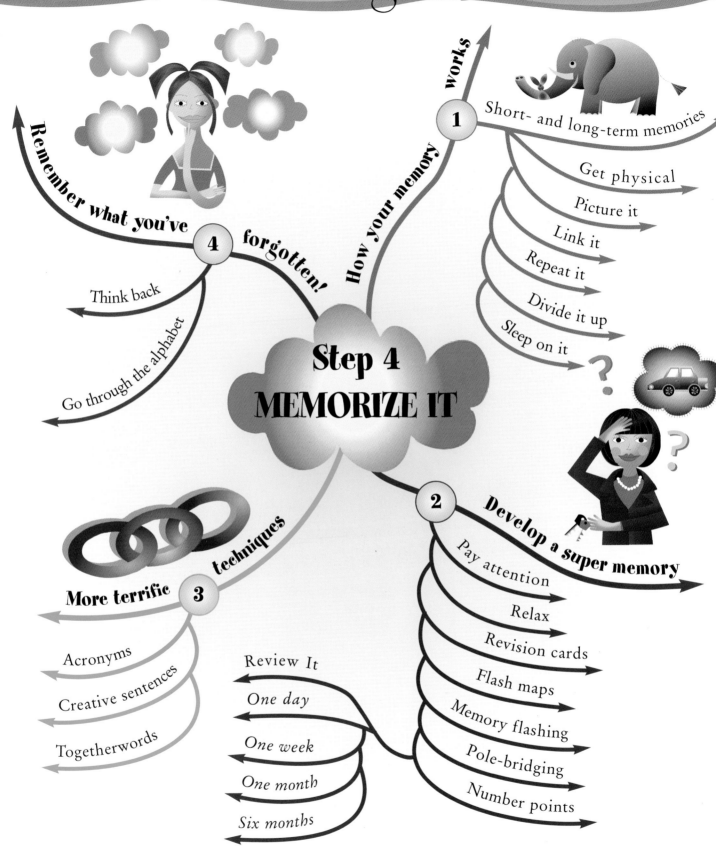

Step 4 MEMORIZE IT

How your memory works
1. Short- and long-term memories
Get physical
Picture it
Link it
Repeat it
Divide it up
Sleep on it

Develop a super memory
2. Pay attention
Relax
Revision cards
Flash maps
Memory flashing
Pole-bridging
Number points

Review It
One day
One week
One month
Six months

More terrific techniques
3. Acronyms
Creative sentences
Togetherwords

Remember what you've forgotten!
4. Think back
Go through the alphabet

Step 5
PROVE YOU KNOW

The only mistake you make is the one you don't learn from. The person who does not make mistakes, does not make anything.

Introduction

Wouldn't it be great if you could know every question of every exam before the exam? Well, with a little effort and planning you can!

All you have to do is make a habit of asking yourself the sorts of questions that you will eventually be asked in the exam. It's a great way to see tests for what they really are—to show you what you still need to put a little more work into.

In Step 5 of CHAMPS you'll find out some successful ways to prove to yourself that you really have learned the information well.

Once you can prove that to yourself, you can prove it to teachers and examiners.

What makes a chemical reaction take place?

Build a question bank

The only reason you're asked questions—in class or in exams—is to give you the chance to *"prove you know"* it or can do it. Don't wait to be asked by someone else—build your own question bank as you go.

As you read your notes or a book or do your homework, ask yourself these two simple questions:
"What questions would someone ask me to make sure that I really understand this?' 'What am I expected to do with this?"*

What is my skin for?

Why do I feel

• Holds my insides in

• Protects them from the outside world

Jot down your questions on cards or in a little notebook. Then put each answer in a few *key* words on the back of the card or page. That way you can go through your *question bank* every month and see if you still know the answers. And, you can always check the answers.

Guess what?
It only takes a few minutes to check 20 or 30 questions and find the ones you can't easily answer. They're the ones to study up on!

Problems and examples from textbooks
These are usually the *key* points. It's a good idea to spend a little time looking over them and making sure you understand the answers.

Homework
The questions you're given for your homework are often the ones you'll be given for tests and exams. Be sure you know the answers!

The main topics in class
Look for clues from your teacher. You'll often get the feeling that she is going over a subject rather a lot and keeps repeating the main conclusions. She may even jot down a summary on the board. If you're not sure, ask whether this is the *key* point you should know.

Old exam questions
Get hold of some past exam papers early on. You won't be able to answer all the questions, but you'll become familiar with the sorts of questions you may be asked.

Test yourself

Testing yourself isn't scary! In fact, it can be fun! Look on it as a great chance to check what you do know and what you still need to know. Before you do any sort of self-testing, relax and breathe deeply (see page 24). Then you'll get a good supply of oxygen to your brain! Here are some good ways to test yourself.

Study buddy quizzes

A great way of testing yourself is to team up with two other classmates, preferably ones who are also using the *question bank* idea. Ask each other, say, 10 questions. You'll probably find that your friends have some questions that you hadn't thought of. And they'll find you have questions they hadn't thought of. The same goes for the answers!

Grade your own homework!

Get in the habit of grading your *own* work. When you finish a piece of homework, say to yourself, "*What grade would I give this?*" If it's below your best—don't hand it in yet. Think about how you can improve it. Then do it!

Check! Check! Check!

It's great to get your work finished. And it's tempting to put in the last full stop on a piece of homework and then forget it! But you haven't quite finished! If you talk to any CHAMP—a writer, a scientist, a teacher, or a business person—they'll tell you that checking what they've done is a major part of their success. Not many people get things absolutely right first time!

Coach's Hot Tip

Make a habit of going back over your work. Is all the spelling correct? Did you say exactly what you wanted?

How many different kinds of clouds are there?

There are cirrus, cumulus, stratus, and nimbostatus clouds!

And there are cirrostratus, cirrocumulus, and cumulonimbus clouds!

Revision cards

Remember those *review cards*—the index cards you created with just the *key words* or *bullet points* written on them? Well, it's a good idea to go through them once a month. This works for all subjects.

- *Can you remember those math or science formulas?*
- *Can you remember those French words?* (The ones you wrote on one side of a card with their meanings in English on the other side.)

HOW MUCH? COMBIEN?

UN POULET CHICKEN

UN LIVRE A BOOK

UN CUILLER A SPOON

- *What were those key dates in history?*

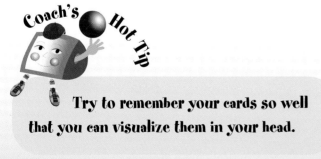

Coach's Hot Tip

Try to remember your cards so well that you can visualize them in your head.

Quel temps fait-il?

Il fait beau!

Oui, il fait chaud!

Make a mental movie

Another good way to *"prove you know"* is to picture yourself using what you've learned. Imagine yourself having a conversation in the language you're learning. Talk out loud, using lots of gestures and facial expressions. You could also run through a sequence from a science subject in your head, or the main events from a period in history.

Making a mental movie involves your feelings so you remember better. You can use this memory technique for anything you do!

Faults or findings

When you're testing yourself, you're bound to make mistakes at some point. Look on them as *"findings"* not *"faults"*. You've found out where there's a problem and you can find out what you need to do about it.

Mistakes are just staging posts on the road to success.

Practice makes perfect

Remember when you were small, you repeated things over and over again? That's because, when you practice something, you give your brain and body lots of opportunity to make sense of the information it's receiving—and to switch it from your short-term to your long-term memory.

To become a learning CHAMP you need to practice the CHAMPS techniques over and over again. Then you won't even need to think about how to do them. Here are two great ways to practice:

Act it out

It really helps you to remember if you act out what you're learning. Talk out loud and use lots of gestures.

Practice in your head!

Remember you found out that your brain can't tell the difference between what is actually happening and what you are imagining.
(If you're frightened of spiders, you'll be just as scared if you imagine one!)

So regularly put down your book and think about the sense of what you have read in your head.

ACTING WORKS BECAUSE:

- You remember and **understand** much more of what you **do** than of what you **read**—because you are actively involved.

- You have created "muscle memory" for what you are learning.

PRACTICING IN YOUR HEAD WORKS BECAUSE:

- You're creating a visual memory of the topic.
- You don't need any equipment.
- You can do it anywhere.

Did you know?
It helps to teach or explain to someone else what you have learned! When you talk about it, you begin to remember it!

This is a really useful technique because you can use your imagination to *"prove you know"*. Sports CHAMPS do this all the time. They practice each movement in their heads until it's right. They also practice winning! You can do it too!

Use it—quickly!

You can only *"prove to yourself"* that you have really understood and learned a new skill when you actually begin to use it—or can use it in a different situation. For example, once you know how to make an electrical circuit, you can use this new knowledge and skill to make different types of circuits.

Fix it in your mind!

Do you remember that on average, you can forget 75 percent of what you learn today by tomorrow night—unless you do something to fix it in your mind? The same is true of learning skills.

Unless you practice a skill right away, it never gets fixed in your mind. So, to make the techniques and ideas in this book really stick, you need to *"remind yourself to use them"*.

Remind yourself to use them!

Throughout this book, you have been told to try out the techniques that suit the way you like to learn. When you have decided on a number of new learning techniques:

- Put up some "post-it" notes of them to *"remind yourself to use them"*.
- Or make a huge *learning map* of all the CHAMPS techniques and stick it on the wall where you do your homework.

The ideas work but *only* if you use them!

See how your friends use them

Talk about all these different learning methods with your friends. *What's working for them? What are their favorite techniques?* Then give them a try. They may well have ideas that you hadn't thought of. Or short cuts.

Coaches

All top athletes have coaches—usually older people who are CHAMPS at their sport. Coaches help by noticing what an athlete can do to improve his or her technique. So it's a good idea to get yourself a coach too!

Using a coach is simple. All you have to do is ask these simple questions:

- *"What do I need to do to become better at this subject?"*
- *"I'm having a bit of trouble with my work— what should I do to solve the problem?"*

You may need different coaches for different subjects—your first stop is your teacher.

Your teachers

Your teachers spend a lot of time at home marking your work. If they take the trouble to comment on your work, you should take the trouble to take note of what they say, and act on it. Teachers are flattered to be asked for help. So if you're confused about something, don't keep struggling—ask!

Your parents

Most parents are great at explaining, so ask them for help. You could *"swap"* places and teach them something too!

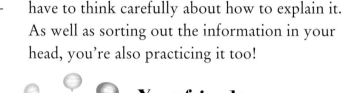

Your brothers and sisters

When you teach new information to younger brothers or sisters, you really have to think carefully about how to explain it. As well as sorting out the information in your head, you're also practicing it too!

Your friends

If you're both studying the same topic, work together with a friend. It helps because you get a great exchange of ideas and you can each find out extra information and teach it to each other.

Ask an expert

Real experts love to share their knowledge with others. The Internet has thousands of different experts that anyone can get in touch with!

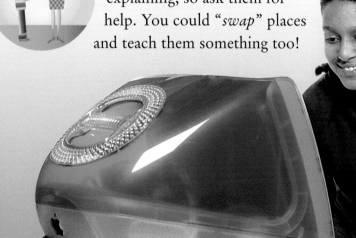

Awesome essays

Throughout school you'll be judged on your written answers to questions in subjects like history, biology, English, and science. You'll get grades for both *what* you write about and *how* you write about it. The secret is to concentrate on getting the *content* right first—and then edit and polish the *style* of your writing afterward. Good writing involves about *40%* research and preparation, about *20%* actual writing and about *40%* editing—or polishing.

Research and rough notes

When you have your notes together try *creative mapping*. Creative maps are like learning maps.

Creating a creative map

1. Put the title in the middle and write down all the ideas and *key* words that come into your head. Use one branch for each main idea.

2. Sit back and look at your *creative map*. Now start to put ideas together in groups. Check back—do they answer the question?

3. Decide what will be in the three parts that every essay needs—a *beginning*, a *middle*, and an *end*.

- The *beginning* sets the scene and makes your reader want to read on.
- The *middle* develops your arguments and ideas. (Remember to back them up with examples, facts, quotations, and evidence.)
- The *end* provides a clever answer to the original question, and ties up any loose ends.

WRITE DRAFT
(20%)

3 BEGINNING
sets scene (last if using computer)

1 MIDDLE
develops ideas (1st)

2 END
summary of answer to question (2nd)

Group ideas

RESEARCH (40%)

Make initial creative map

AWESOME ESSAYS

2 Style

EDIT (NEXT DAY) – (40%)

Subheads?

Short sentences?

Paragraphs for each new idea?

Read it aloud

Does it answer the question?

Spell check

Good examples?

Punchy opening?

Books

Internet

CD-ROMS

1 Content

CREATIVE MAP

Awesome essays

Draft it

Now, start to write—you start with the *middle*!! If possible, use a computer—that way you can move text around, cut, and paste.

Bands of fierce Viking warriors have sailed south in their warships to steal, kill , and trade. They have met Arabs with their caravans of camels carrying fine silk and other rare things to sell.

- Remember to give each new idea it's own paragraph.
- Don't worry too much about style or spelling at this stage.
- Look at your *creative map* and write up each main group of ideas, one by one.

When you've finished your draft of the *middle*, it's time to write your *ending*.

- Check your ending sums up your answer to the question.
- Look back at the draft of your *middle*.
- Jot down the 10 most important *key* words.
- Find the shortest way to link them together —that's your *ending*.

Now draft the *beginning*—it'll give your reader the "*big picture*" of what you're going to say.

> **Remember! Your beginning is the first thing your teachers (or examiners) see. A good beginning will put them in a good mood!!**

Finally, sleep on it, if you have the time! If you walk away from your essay for a few hours, you'll find that you'll see points you missed or things you could write better when you come back.

Edit it

Now think about style.

- Is the meaning clear?
- Have you used words that really describe what you mean?

Read your essay out loud.

- Does it sound good?
- Have you used subheadings that make it easy to read?
- Have you given examples to bring your ideas to life?

Now pay attention to the beginning.

- Does it start with a bang?
- Does it make the reader want to read more?
- Keep your sentences short—long sentences are difficult to understand.

The last thing to do is to edit the ending.

- Really think about it.
- Is it punchy enough?

Coach's Hot Tip

RULES TO GOOD WRITING:

- Check what you are being asked to write about. Read the question two or three times.
- Gather together the information you need— the Internet might be a good place to start.
- Plan the answer in your head.
- Write up the answer in rough first.
- Edit your rough draft so it's as good as it can possibly be.

Be an exam expert

Up until now you haven't had to think too much about exams. But they are a way of life in secondary school, so it's a good idea to know now how to plan for them in advance.

Revision reminders

Revision can sometimes be difficult to organize as there's often so much to do. It's best to break it down into manageable chunks, like this:

Remember!

Allow time to test yourself on each topic for 5 minutes every evening and every morning. This can more than double how much you remember!

BEFORE YOU BEGIN TO REVISE, REMEMBER THESE THINGS:

- Revise similar subjects on different days—if they are too similar you can muddle them up.
- Study with friends who are serious about learning.
- Use study guides and past papers to guide you on the sorts of questions you're likely to be asked.
- Manage your time—decide what's important and make a "to do" list.
- Keep a note of what you've done.
- Take regular breaks—revise for 30 minutes at a time—and then take a 5-minute break.
- Remember your review program—on the day you review a topic, revise your notes again quickly for about 5 minutes before you go to sleep. Then do another quick 5-minute revision on that subject the next morning.

- Look at your goals and repeat your affirmations.
- Exercise in between revision sessions.
- Remember, you can revise anywhere.
- Don't leave it too late!
- Eat brain food and drink lots of water.
- Get enough sleep.
- Keep cool!

Planning for exams

Revising for an exam is a little different from normal revision. It's about getting ready for a particular date that's several weeks or even months ahead.

A GOOD WAY TO PLAN FOR YOUR EXAMS IS TO:

Make a list of the topics that you will need to know thoroughly (check with your teacher).

3 weeks	2 weeks
1 week	EXAM!

Work back from the exam date—how many weeks have you got?

Write down the topic or topics you will revise each week. Remember, you need to have revised them all by two weeks before the exam.

Allow time in your weekly list to test yourself on each topic for five minutes every evening and every morning.

Check off each topic as you finish revising it. (That'll make you feel good!)

MICROBES
1. Skin and eyes
2. Digestive system
3. Respiratory system
4. Reproductive system
5. Vectors (mosquitos, fleas)

The two spare weeks before the exam is for revising the topics you don't remember as well. Get your revision cards out for these topics.

Keep looking away from these cards and summarizing the key points out loud in your own words. If you find that a revision card doesn't answer all the questions you might be asked, go to your textbook and add that information.

Don't forget to plan those rewards!!

Coach's Hot Tip

The big advantage of exam and action plans is that you feel confident and in control. And you don't get caught out in a panic!

Be an exam expert

Exams can seem pretty scary so you need to be well prepared and feel confident that you will be successful. Here's a checklist to help you:

1. Before the exam
- If possible, have a look at the room where you'll be taking your exam.
- Sit at a desk and visualize yourself answering all the questions easily.

2. The evening before
- Check that you have all the equipment you need and that it's all in working order!
- Have an early night.

3. Morning of exam
- Get up early.
- Have a good stretch or go for a brisk walk.
- Have a high-energy breakfast with plenty of water or juice.
- Take a bottle of water with you.
- Leave in plenty of time but don't get to school too early.

4. When you get there
- Believe in yourself and feel the confidence inside you.
- Relax and breathe deeply for a couple of minutes.
- Massage your temples to relax you even more.
- Sit with a positive attitude —as if you really mean business!

5. Follow instructions
- Listen carefully to the examiner's instructions.
- Make sure that you have filled in your personal details correctly.
- Read the whole paper first.
- Read each question slowly and carefully and decide which ones to do.
- Re-read each question carefully.
- Highlight instructions.

6. Answers
- Plan using learning maps, bullet points, or diagrams.
- For a 3-hour exam you would expect to spend at least 30 minutes reading the questions and planning.
- See the "answers" in your head.
- Write neatly.
- For math or science subjects, always show step-by-step workings or planning notes.

- Keep an eye on the clock.
- Talk positively to yourself.
- Answer the easiest and shortest questions first.
- Stretch and breathe deeply in between each answer.
- Don't stick on a question and run out of time—come back to it later.

7. When you have finished
- Quickly glance over your answers.
- Check that you've answered the right number of questions.

Learning map

Step 5 — PROVE YOU KNOW

1. Build a question bank
- Class topics
- Homework clues
- Old exam questions
- Textbook examples

2. Test yourself

- Study buddy quizzes
- Mark your homework
- Check! Check! Check!
- Revision cards
- Mental movies
- Mistakes can help

3. Practice makes perfect
- Act it out
- Practice in your head
- Explain to someone else
- Remind yourself
- Post-it notes
- Learning maps

4. Get a coach

- Your teachers
- Your parents
- Your brothers and sisters
- Your friends
- Ask an expert

5. Awesome essays
Middle first
Ending second
Beginning last
- Research
- Rough notes
- Map the outline
- Draft it
- Edit it

6. Be an exam expert
- Revision reminders
- List topics
- Plan revision
- Go through review
- Check off topics
- Exam tips
- Highlight instructions
- Plan the answer
- Show workings
- Move on

Step 6

SIT BACK AND THINK

You cannot teach a man anything.
You can only help him discover it within himself.

C.H.A.M.P.S.

Now you know about 5 of the CHAMPS steps . . .

C **onfident to learn**
Getting your mind and body ready to learn.

H **ome in on the facts**
Taking in the information memorably.

A **ction!**
Thinking deeply so you understand that information.

M **emorize it**
Remembering what you have learned.

P **rove you know**
Showing yourself and others what you have learned.

S **it back and think**
This is the final step—Step 6 of CHAMPS.

Step 6 will teach you how important it is, now you know some great learning techniques, that you don't just automatically think you're going to become a learning CHAMP. It's time to think more deeply about what CHAMPS means—what it can do for you and what you will do with it!

Picture yourself using one or two of the CHAMPS techniques for a few minutes. If you need to, glance back through the book to remind yourself. Now tackle Step 6—"Sit back and think"—how you feel about what you know so far!

Reflect on it

You *think* about what you've been doing when you ask two simple questions: *What went well? What could I have done better?* This is called *reflecting* and it's a very important skill. People who don't *think* about what they have been doing are likely to make the same mistakes over and over again.

All successful people take the time to *think* carefully about the techniques they use—which are working best and which need some improvement. *You* need to do that too! So, *sit back—and think*. Not about *what* you learned, but about *how* you learned it.

Remember!
Asking yourself questions puts your brain into "search mode."

The only place where success comes before either "thought" or "work" is in the dictionary!!

FOR EACH OF THE IDEAS OR LEARNING TECHNIQUES YOU HAVE CHOSEN, ASK YOURSELF THESE QUESTIONS:

- Have I tried out this technique yet?
- What happened—was it useful?
- Will I use this often in the future?
- What did I really enjoy doing?
- What was I good at? Can I do more of that?
- What did I have difficulty with?
- Should I practice more?
- What do I want to improve?
- How can I do that?

You see the point. You get **better** when you *think* about or *reflect* on how you are doing and whether you can do it better next time.

Coach's Hot Tip

You can work hard in the wrong way and achieve little. Or you can work smart using the right techniques and achieve a lot—with much less effort.

Use it!

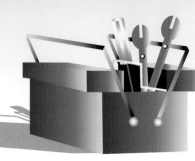

The 6 steps of CHAMPS are really
like having a box of useful *"tools"* that will
make your work easier and help you get to the top.
But equipment and tools need to be well cared for
and used or they won't work! If you don't use the *"tools"*
and keep them *"sharp"*, they'll become rusty and useless!

It's the same with CHAMPS—it's a learning
course that you don't just work through
once—it's for you to come back to again
and again. It'll help you when things get
a bit tough at school. And when things are
going well and you want to do even better!

So really practice and use as many of these
learning techniques as you can. You could
also compare the ones you like best to
the ones that your friends like best
and then teach each other your
favorite techniques.

YOU REALLY WILL BENEFIT FROM THE CHAMPS TECHNIQUES BECAUSE:

- You can use them now
- At home
- At college
- At your next school
- In your new job
- In fact—for the rest of your life!

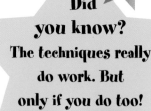

**Did
you know?**
The techniques really
do work. But
only if you do too!

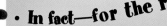

Keep a "learning log"

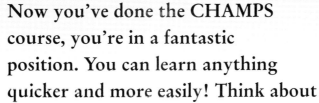

Now you've done the CHAMPS course, you're in a fantastic position. You can learn anything quicker and more easily! Think about it. You've got lots of techniques for learning that will enable you to learn by yourself— independently, that is!

If it's to be, it's up to me!!

A good idea to help you become an independent learner is to keep your own *learning log*. A learning log is simply a note book where you record your thoughts about learning.

Coach's Hot Tip

REMEMBER! "Use it, or lose it!"

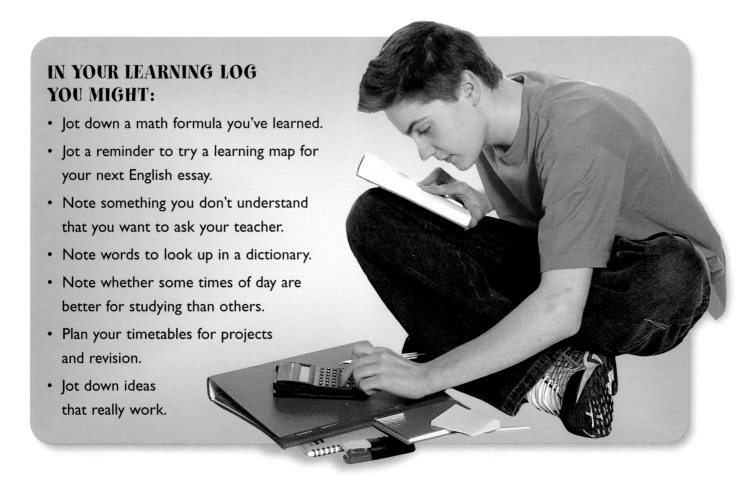

IN YOUR LEARNING LOG YOU MIGHT:

- Jot down a math formula you've learned.

- Jot a reminder to try a learning map for your next English essay.

- Note something you don't understand that you want to ask your teacher.

- Note words to look up in a dictionary.

- Note whether some times of day are better for studying than others.

- Plan your timetables for projects and revision.

- Jot down ideas that really work.

Push your comfort zone

Now you've found out about using techniques that suit the way that you like to learn—that suit your learning style best. It does make sense to concentrate on those first, because you get good results straight away.

The more techniques you have, the more able you are to tackle anything in the future. So once you've started to see some real improvements in your learning, look back through CHAMPS and try out as many other ideas as you can. That's what's called, *"pushing your comfort zone"*.

Think about the sorts of people who are successful.

- *What happens to them when they become successful?*
- *Do they sit back and rest? Do they sit back quietly and think about what they are going to do next?*

No, they don't, and here's why!

The purpose of education is to replace an empty mind with an open one.

Why do they bother?

Because if you just stay where you are, you get bored and you don't have to use your brain. When you don't use your brain, you lose its power!

Coach's Hot Tip

Even adults need to keep moving forward so that they keep their brains working properly.

SUCCESSFUL PEOPLE:

- Are never satisfied
- Don't sit still
- Keep moving forward
- Continue to become even more expert at what they do
- Keep setting themselves new challenges and goals

You've done brilliantly to complete the CHAMPS course and you should be very pleased with yourself.

BUT REMEMBER!

YOU NEED TO DO THE SAME THING AS ANY SUPER CHAMP:

- Don't be satisfied

- Don't sit still

- Keep moving forward

- Continue to practice and improve your learning skills

- Keep setting yourself new challenges and goals

Guess what? Then you really will become a super **learning CHAMP** too!

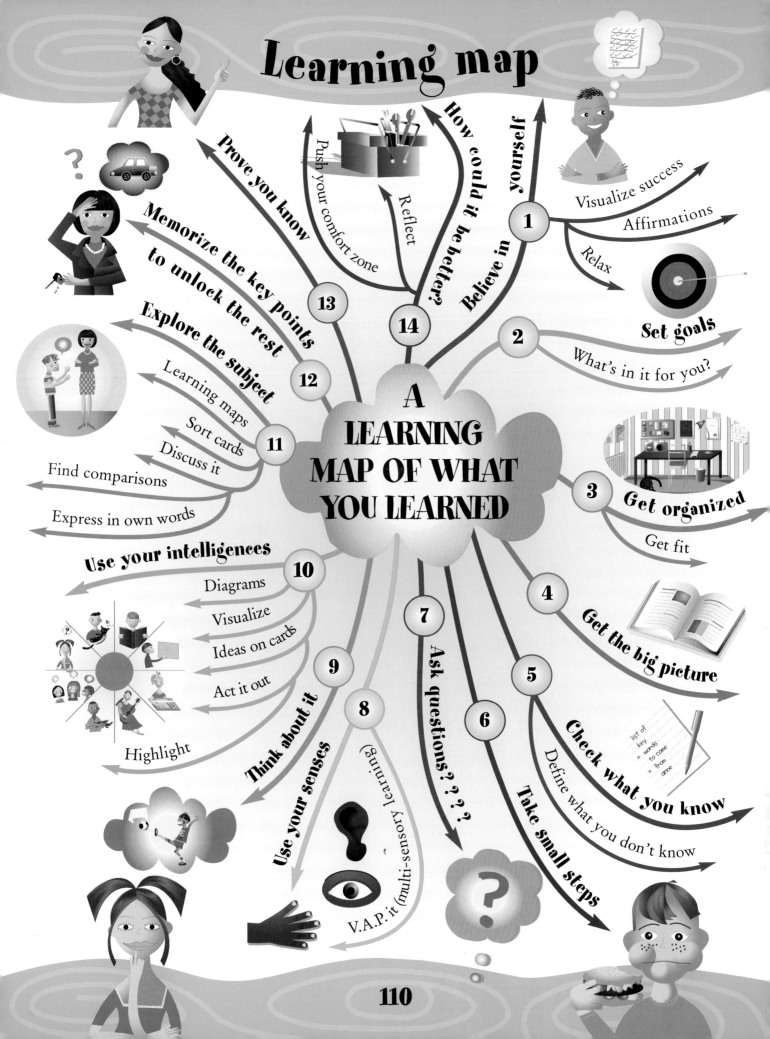

Learning map

Learning CHAMPS - on-line

The ideal companion to Learning CHAMPS is CHAMPS—an Internet-delivered learning-to-learn course for students.

There is a separate CHAMPS on-line course for 10-13 year-olds and one for 14-17 year-old students. (And even one for adults at work—because learning faster and remembering more is a competitive advantage for companies as well as students!)

The CHAMPS web-based course extends Learning CHAMPS by providing further learning and memory techniques and lots of examples of all the techniques in practice— examples that are directly relevant to the subjects the student is studying. Students can do an interactive test to assess their preferred way of learning and print out the results—together with all the learning techniques they have decided to use.

Individual students can purchase access to the on-line course or a CD-ROM version. Schools can buy site licence.

See it at **www.learningchamps.com** **<http://www.learningchamps.com>** for individual use and **www.learntolearn.org** **<http://www.learntolearn.org>** for schools.

See also **www.acceleratedlearning.com** **<http://www.acceleratedlearning.com>** for innovative programs for learning foreign languages—including Spanish, French, and German on-line.

Index